AF279413

English Pronunciation: A Manual to Understand and Communicate Effectively

Colección MANUALES #84: Textos Universitarios 33

ENGLISH PRONUNCIATION:
A MANUAL TO UNDERSTAND AND COMMUNICATE EFFECTIVELY

Eva Pelayo Sañudo

Pelayo Sañudo, Eva, autor
    English pronunciation : a manual to understand and communicate effectively /
Eva Pelayo Sañudo. – Santander : Editorial de la Universidad de Cantabria, [D.L.
2023]
    116 páginas : ilustraciones ; 24 cm. – (Manuales ; 84. Textos universitarios ; 33)

    D.L. SA 642-2023. – ISBN 978-84-19024-56-5

1. Inglés (Lengua)-Pronunciación

811.111'355

THEMA: CJ, 2ACB, 4CT, YPCK21

Maquetación | digitalización: Manuel Ángel Ortiz Velasco [emeaov]
Imagen de cubierta: Ricardo Ortiz Recio

© Eva Pelayo Sañudo [Universidad de Cantabria]
   https://orcid.org/0000-0003-2786-5437
© Editorial de la Universidad de Cantabria
   Avda. de los Castros, 52 - 39005 Santander. Cantabria (España)
   Tlfno.: +34 942 201 087
   ISNI: https://isni.org/isni/0000000506860180
   www.editorial.unican.es

ISBN: 978-84-19024-56-5 (RÚSTICA)
D.L.: SA 642-2023
ISBN: 978-84-19024-57-2 (PDF)
DOI: https://doi.org/10.22429/Euc2023.028

Impreso en España-*Printed in Spain*
Imprime: Estugraf impresores S.L.

INDEX

PREFACE

Este Manual se origina a partir de una ayuda recibida en la I Convocatoria de Generación de Recursos Audiovisuales, del Vicerrectorado de Títulos Propios y Enseñanza a Distancia de la Universidad de Cantabria, dentro del proyecto titulado *Didáctica de la pronunciación de la lengua inglesa: Diseño y elaboración de material didáctico para mejorar la competencia lingüística en asignaturas de lengua inglesa.*

Una fase de este proyecto pretende compilar el material elaborado en un Manual para su uso por parte del profesorado de asignaturas de lengua inglesa en la Universidad de Cantabria. Dado que la pronunciación es un componente fundamental en el conocimiento de la lengua inglesa, el Manual puede ser de utilidad en distintos grados de la universidad, independientemente de los contenidos específicos que se impartan en una titulación dada. En otras palabras, tiene relevancia tanto para las asignaturas de lengua inglesa de la Facultad de Económicas y Empresariales como para las Ingenierías o la rama de las Ciencias de la Salud.

El objetivo principal es introducir la enseñanza o el aprendizaje formal de la pronunciación y que el alumnado adquiera una serie de conocimientos básicos sobre fonética para así mejorar de manera sustancial las destrezas orales y de forma global su competencia lingüística en lengua inglesa. En general, el alumnado que cursa asignaturas de lengua inglesa en nuestra universidad (con un nivel en torno al A2-B1) tiene pocas nociones de las diferencias de sonidos que existen entre la lengua propia y la lengua meta, lo que constituye un elemento imprescindible no solo a la hora de comprender los mensajes de hablantes nativos de la lengua inglesa sino también para hacerse comprender adecuadamente. De hecho, es necesario alcanzar unos estándares mínimos de pronunciación (lo que se denomina un "*thereshold level*") pues de otro modo la calidad del habla de una persona podría interferir en sus habilidades para comunicarse a pesar de que ya domine la gramática y el vocabulario de la lengua (Celce-Murcia *et al.* 2010, p. 8).

Por ello, se busca que el alumnado domine o corrija su pronunciación mediante el conocimiento de las reglas y particularidades fonéticas del inglés, las cuales, al igual que otros aspectos de la lengua como la gramática o el vocabulario, han de ser explicadas y estudiadas expresamente. Este conocimiento básico de la lengua, particularmente a la hora de comunicar(se) de forma apropiada, será abordado a través de una serie de contenidos que recogen de forma concisa y práctica los principales elementos sobre pronunciación, incluyendo las múltiples diferencias de sonidos entre el inglés y el español.

En definitiva, este Manual tiene una aplicación transversal en todas las asignaturas de lengua inglesa de la Universidad de Cantabria y resulta de interés para la inmersión lingüística como complemento a la instrucción académica dentro del aula. Especialmente, se potencia el desarrollo de las destrezas orales (*speaking y listening*). Así, la falta de tiempo para abordar la pronunciación o para la previa preparación de materiales por parte del profesorado no deberían ser un impedimento ya que los recursos existentes permiten fácilmente adaptar la instrucción a las necesidades oportunas (Cox *et al.* 2019) y teniendo en cuenta las implicaciones pedagógicas en que se centran hoy en día los estudios sobre pronunciación de una segunda lengua o lengua extranjera (Derwing y Munro 2005; Kirkova-Naskova 2021).

Además, el Manual tendría relevancia en los Postgrados en Aprendizaje y Enseñanza de lenguas impartidos en la Facultad de Educación (Máster en Formación del Profesorado de Educación Secundaria y Máster en Aprendizaje y Enseñanza de Segundas Lenguas); dada la experiencia docente a lo largo de los años así como numerosas investigaciones del campo de la enseñanza y de la adquisición de lenguas, aún resulta necesario fomentar el aprendizaje de la fonética en las aulas, la cual es o ha sido tradicionalmente ignorada incluso como parte fundamental en las destrezas orales y los objetivos comunicativos (Morley 1991, p. 485; Celce Murcia *et al.* 1996, p. 323; Jones 1997, p. 105; Levis 2006, p. 245; Isaacs y Trofimovich 2016, p. 4; Calvo-Benzies 2016, pp. 120-124).

Esta atención al componente fonético es particularmente importante en estadios más tempranos en que se aprende la lengua inglesa pues, de otro modo, es frecuente que se fosilicen errores y que haya malentendidos o problemas en futuras situaciones de comunicación. En otras palabras, el conocimiento de la pronunciación no debería estar restringido a los estudios especializados (p. ej. al Grado de Estudios Ingleses o la Mención en Lengua Extranjera del Grado de Magisterio), sino que ha de ser transversal a cualquier asignatura que se imparta en inglés puesto que la fonética y la fonología conforman una parte integral del aprendizaje y dominio de la lengua inglesa.

INTRODUCTION

I.   PERCEPTION AND PRODUCTION

Perception not only accompanies but precedes production or as David Nunan puts it "begin with comprehension before production" (2015, p. 98). An important aspect to clarify is that learning to pronounce properly means, first and foremost, a proper understanding in terms of listening or perception. To start with, it is very difficult you can produce a sound you cannot perceive first. It is important that students are taught how to recognize the different phonemes or sounds of the target language (English in this case), as well as discriminate between the sound system of English and Spanish.

For example, Spanish speakers may have intelligibility problems as there are phonemes which are not present in their own language (e.g., several vowels) while other sounds may be similar but not exactly the same and cause frequent misunderstandings (e.g., the consonants /s/ and /z/). The same applies to suprasegmental features, that is, additional differences beyond individual sounds (or segmental components) in terms of rhythm, stress and intonation. To avoid intelligibility problems both in terms of understanding or perception (as we fail to hear certain sounds) and production (as we cannot pronounce sounds we do not know or have in our language), it is necessary to have some basic knowledge of pronunciation and learn the International Phonetic Alphabet (IPA), which is just as useful as the Latin Alphabet we all use to read and write.

Once students learn the main pronunciation differences in both languages and can perceive them properly (e.g. recognize how two phonemes sound differently), they should have no problems in pronouncing correctly by remembering those sounds differences and practicing as much as possible. Therefore, this book concentrates on perceptive and productive skills both at a segmental and suprasegmental level.

II.   SPELLING vs SOUNDS

Another essential difference is that, **in English, the spelling (grapheme) is usually different from the pronunciation (phoneme)**. For example, the same spelling or grapheme ("u") corresponds to more than one sound: *put:* /pʊt/[1]; *cut:* /kʌt/[2]. By contrast, in Spanish there is a one-to-one correspondence between graphemes/letters and phonemes/sounds, and the pronunciation of words can be predicted from their spelling. Whereas "a" is always pronounced as /a/ in Spanish, look at all the possible sounds of "a" in English: Letter/grapheme "a" ➜ phoneme/sound: /æ/, /ɑ:/, /ɒ/, /ɔ:/, /ə/, /ɪ/, /eɪ/, /eə/

plan: /æ/	*watch:* /ɒ/	*about:* /ə/	*plane:* /eɪ/
example: /ɑ:/	*tall:* /ɔ:/	*village:* /ɪ/	*scary:* /eə/

---

[1] The slashes / / are a convention used to write the pronunciation of a word or letter, that is, the phonemes. In turn, graphemes are indicated by the use of inverted commas: "".

[2] Look at the Sound bank in Annex 1 to learn the different graphemes that can be associated to each of the phonemes in English. Notice: learning the most frequent spellings for each sound (what can be called *spelling rules*) can help you predict the pronunciation of most words.

Spanish speakers also have a tendency to pronounce all the letters that appear in the spelling. There are 26 letters in the English alphabet but there are many more sounds in the English language: 44. This means that the number of sounds in a word is not always the same as the number of letters or graphemes. For example, the word *cat* has three letters and three sounds, but the word *catch* has five letters but only three sounds (the letters "tch" correspond only to one sound, /tʃ/). If we write these words using sound symbols, we will know how many sounds they have: /kæt/ vs /kætʃ/.

Finally, not all letters are pronounced in English words, as in *cupboard*, where there is no /p/: /ˈkʌbəd/[3]. These are silent letters. Apart from the "r", which is not generally pronounced (in non-rhotic languages)[4], other silent letters are provided in the following list of commonly used words: *sword, calm, lamb, receipt, sign, soften, debt, **known, psalm, cupboard, wrong, right**.

Most Spanish speakers actually know that English spelling has little or nothing to do with pronunciation. However, as the sounds in the Spanish language are very close to the spelling, it is very common that they tend to reproduce this tendency in English too (linking pronunciation to spelling). This is specially obvious in the cases where Spanish and English words are similar in terms of spelling. Spanish speakers will accurately understand the meaning but will likely fail to notice the pronunciation differences. Listen to some words which are close to Spanish spelling but are pronounced totally differently in English: *euro, peculiar, radio, education, vocabulary, pronunciation.*

As said above, in English there are 26 letters but 44 sounds and sometimes it is indeed difficult to know the pronunciation from the spelling. For this reason, Spanish speakers need to forget about the Latin alphabet which we use to write and get familiar with the **International Phonetic Alphabet,** that is, the symbols that represent the sounds we need to understand and pronounce (such as /ʌ/, /ŋ/, /ð/ and many others)[5]. In this way, they will be able to read a phonetic transcription (the pronunciation) of any word or sentence and avoid being misled by spelling.

Furthermore, knowing the phonetic symbols is useful so that you can check the pronunciation of new words in any dictionary. Using **pronunciation dictionaries** (e.g., *Cambridge English Pronunciation Dictionary* or *Longman Pronunciation Dictionary*) is particularly recommended as they include more words than general dictionaries, so you can check the pronunciation of toponyms (place names), family and brand names and technical terms.

---

[3] ' is the mark used to indicate stress in words with more than one syllable (in the examples *table* and *baseball*, the first syllable); monosyllabic words are all stressed so the mark is often redundant. This content will be covered in Unit 5.

[4] Notice: American English is called a 'rhotic' accent, which means that the "r" is pronounced (as it is in Ireland, Wales and Scotland). By contrast, RP English is 'non-rhotic'.

[5] You will learn all the symbols of English sounds along the different units of this Manual, but you can find a list of all the vowel and consonant sounds in Annex 2.

One useful exercise is to start with inverse **transcription**, that is, practicing with easy transcriptions and trying to guess the word you are reading until you gradually identify all the symbols, e.g. if you read /'teɪbəl/ or /'beɪsbəl/, you will probably recognize the words *table* and *baseball* even if you do not know the symbol /ə/, which probably you will read it as the Spanish /e/ or /a/ respectively; a more difficult word could be /'dɔːtə/, which is spelt *daughter*, where the letters "au" correspond to a vowel similar to Spanish "o" (but longer) and the final "r" is not pronounced. To read and recognize other transcribed words such as /tʃuːz/ (*choose*), you will need to know that the symbol /tʃ/ corresponds to the spelling "ch", as well as familiarize with the consonant /z/, which is often confused with Spanish /s/ and creates misunderstandings. It is very important that you read aloud the transcriptions; if you actually hear them you will recognize more easily the words[6]. Here is an example of the type of exercises of inverse transcription available which are helpful for you to start identifying the phonetic symbols (see also Annex 7 for extra practice).

Sam the Spy likes to send messages in phonetic code. Can you decode the names of countries from his Phonetic Code Book? Match the words in the box with the words in phonetic code.

Argentina	Australia	Austria	Brazil
England	France	Germany	Greece
Hungary	Italy	Poland	Turkey

1 /ˈɪŋglənd/
   England

5 /ˈdʒɜːmənɪ/

9 /ˈtɜːkɪ /

2 /ˈpəʊlənd/

6 /frɑːns/

10 /ˈhʌŋgərɪ/

3 /ˈɒstrɪə/

7 /griːs/

11 /ɑːdʒənˈtiːnə/

4 /ɒstˈreɪlɪə/

8 /ˈɪtəlɪ/

12 /brəˈzɪl/

Inverse transcription exercice from *Timesaver Pronunciation Activities* (2005), by Bill Bowler, p. 40

---

[6] A complete list of the sound symbols is given on the section about the IPA in the interactive exercises of Annex 7 where you can click on each sound to hear it; it includes some extra exercises of inverse transcription (from sound to spelling) to help you learn the symbols.

Listen to further advice about why we need the IPA; it is recommended that the best way to improve pronunciation is to learn each different sound of English, for which it is necessary to learn the symbols.

In summary, rely on sound symbols rather than letters or spelling of words. The pronunciation of the word *bed* is written /bed/. In this particular example, the sound symbols look exactly the same as the letters or graphemes. You can only know that it refers to pronunciation rather than spelling because of the use of / /. However, generally words look very different when you see their pronunciation: /tʃ3:tʃ/ is the word *church*. This is why it is worthy learning the phonetic symbols.

III.   WHICH ENGLISH?

Although there are many varieties of English, this Manual concentrates on the so-called RP (Received Pronunciation) or British English for being a commonly used reference to learn a standard and manageable version of English pronunciation. However, it is also essential to know some important differences of American English (AE) not only as there are as many speakers of AE as of RP but also due to the leading influence of the United States in the world and its important presence in the media (such as cinema, TV or music).

An essential distinctive feature is that the "r" is pronounced in American English as opposed to the British non-rhotic RP. Here are some other important features of AE which are different from RP in terms of pronunciation:[7]

- Intervocalic "t": when "t" appears between vowels (as in *water, butter, writter, city, little*), it is flapped and sounds like Spanish alveolar /r/ (the one in the Spanish word *pera*). Listen to the following examples: *water, better, matter, city, eating.*

---

[7] There are also some differences in terms of spelling, vocabulary and grammar. These differences are not covered in this Manual which focuses on pronunciation.

Compare the following examples in which the words are produced in RP English or American English:

latter: AE   *brighter:* RP
writer: RP   *Betty:* AE
greater: RP   *kettle:*RP
cattle: AE   *letter:* AE

- Cluster "nt" (*twenty*): sounds just /n/.

- Vowel /æ/ rather than /ɑ:/ e.g., *bath, ask, calm, dance, after, can't.*
  Note the pronunciation of *can't* depending on the accent:

	RP	AE
Yes, I can	/kæn/	/kæn/
No, I can't	/kɑ:nt/	/kænt/

- /ɒ/ sounds like Spanish /a/ or like RP /ɔ:/ but produced with a more open mouth:

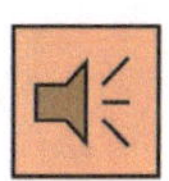 

lot   *lost*
pot   *boss*
watch   *dog*
holiday   *gone*

- Diphthong /əʊ/ sounds /ou/: *so, no, go*. Compare the following words produced with RP /əʊ/ and AE /oʊ/ respectively: *goat, coat, vote, close, load.*

- Stress patterns change in some words: ***address, advertisement.***

- Some specific words are pronounced differently: *tomato* (AE /eɪ/ vs RP /a:/), ***route*** (AE /au/ vs RP /u:/), ***schedule*** (AE /sk/ vs RP /ʃ/).

You can visit Rachel's English if you want to know more about the sounds in American English, with very detailed video-lessons and illustrations. There is a guide (*Free Sounds of American English Cheat Sheet,* 2022) for you to download for free, where the pronunciation of each sound is accompanied by illustrations of her mouth.

Alternatively, for further practice about British English you can watch the different resources presented by Alex Bellem in BBC Learning English. For each sound, there is a short explanatory video which can also be downloaded, and which is very didactic as it allows you to look at her face/mouth closely when she pronounces the sound and words so that students repeat them later.

Furthermore, it is highly recommended to gain exposure to models of pronunciation from native speakers and from language use aside from teachers' instruction (Goodwin 2008), particularly through the available technological and digital resources. As research shows, new technologies not only allow you to understand better the "mechanics of articulation" but also provide you with independent practice and favour autonomous learning (Yoshida 2018, p. 197; Llisterri 2001, p. 21), as well as offer more varied, updated, engaging and real or contextualized materials (Calvo-Benzies 2017, p. 3).

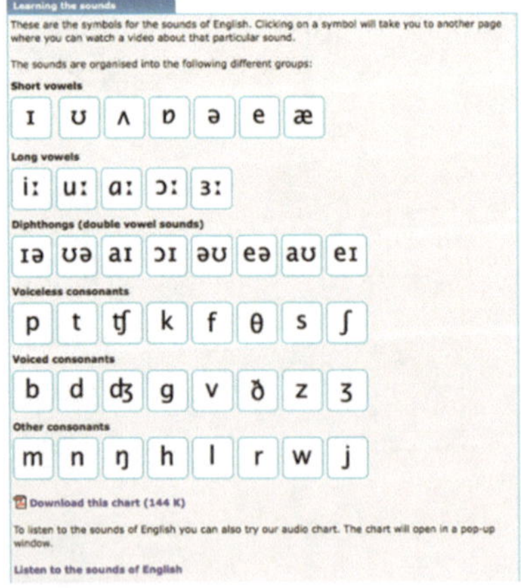

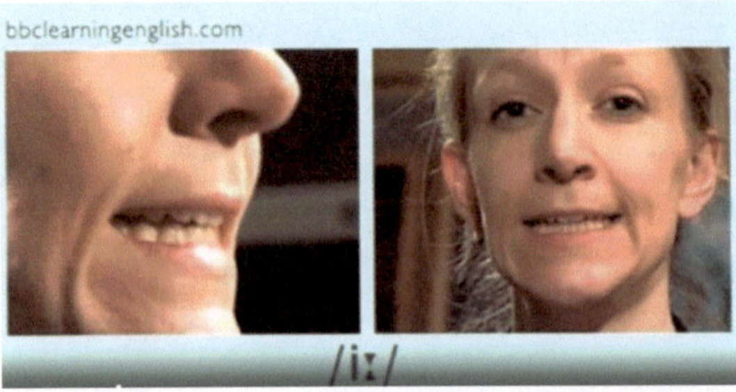

Video guides and resources to learn and practice pronunciation in the websites *Rachel's English* and *BBC Learning English*

1. VOWELS

[TESTING YOUR] PRELIMINARY KNOWLEDGE

Here are some question to reflect on some basic notions of English pronunciation:
1. How many vowel sounds are there in English?
2. Write down the words associated to the pictures below.
3. Can you establish any relationship between the letters/spelling of the words (graphemes) and the phonetic symbols?

Figure 0. Vowel sounds of English (phonetic symbols)

I.   DIFFERENCES BETWEEN THE ENGLISH AND SPANISH VOWEL SYSTEMS

/ɪ/	/iː/	/ʊ/	/uː/
fil	*feel*	*cook*	*moon*
/æ/	/ʌ/	/ɑː/	/ə/
map	*bus*	*car*	*mother*
/e/	/ɜː/	/ɒ/	/ɔː/
pet	*girl*	*clock*	*door*

Figure 1. Vowel sounds of English (phonetic symbols)

[HOW TO AVOID] COMMON MISTAKES

◊ **MIND THE DIFFERENT VOWEL**

Spanish /**a**/ vs English /**æ, ʌ, ɑ:**/

✘ Common mistake:

Ban, bun, barn: Spanish speakers may mispronounce these three English words, all of them with the same vowel, Spanish /a/.

✓ Correct pronunciation: there are three different vowels, namely /bæn/, /bʌn/ and /bɑ:n/.

☞ Explanation: in English there are three **different vowels** (/æ, ʌ, ɑ:/) which resemble our "a" vowel in Spanish. The most common mistake for Spanish speakers is to pronounce the three English words in the example above with the same vowel (the Spanish /a/). Therefore, English speakers will not know whether we are referring to *ban, bun* or *barn* and what we really mean. Most likely, we will be making a mistake. For example, compare these different sentences in which by changing just one vowel you are saying something completely different:

Where is my cap? → /æ/
Where is my cup? → /ʌ/
Where is my carp? → /ɑ:/

◊ **MIND THE LENGTH DIFFERENCE**

Spanish /**e**/ vs English /**ɜ:**/

✘ Common mistake:

Bed or *bird?* Spanish speakers may also mispronounce this pair, even if they know that the vowels are different now. Due to spelling, they might think that the first is pronounced /bed/ and the second /bird/.

✓ Correct pronunciation: /bed/ and /bɜ:d/ do not sound exactly the same although the quality of the vowels is different (/e/ and /ɜ:/). The main difference is the length (in the word *bird*). Students should know that, as a rule, in English /r/ is not pronounced and makes the preceding vowel longer.

☞ Explanation: in English there are several **long vowels**, so it is crucial that Spanish students learn this difference to make the correct sound. Compare again how by changing just one vowel (long for short) you are meaning something completely different: *He's got a big bed at home* vs *He's got a big bird at home; We weren't there* vs *We went there*.

Bear in mind the evidence indicating that "most complex problems for Spanish learners are caused by the distinction between long and short vowels [...] because length is not a distinctive feature in the Spanish vocalic system" (Calvo-Benzies 2013, p. 39). On the other hand, the interference of the native language is particularly evident in the field of pronunciation as compared to other areas of English learning (Gallardo 2008, p. 41). For this reason, it is important that the teaching of pronunciation is as adapted as possible to the learners' expected problems or difficulties.

In this first unit we are going to compare the different vowel systems of English and Spanish. The main difference is that there are **only 5 vowel sounds in Spanish**, whereas **in English there are 12 vowel sounds**, as you can see in the following quadrilaterals:

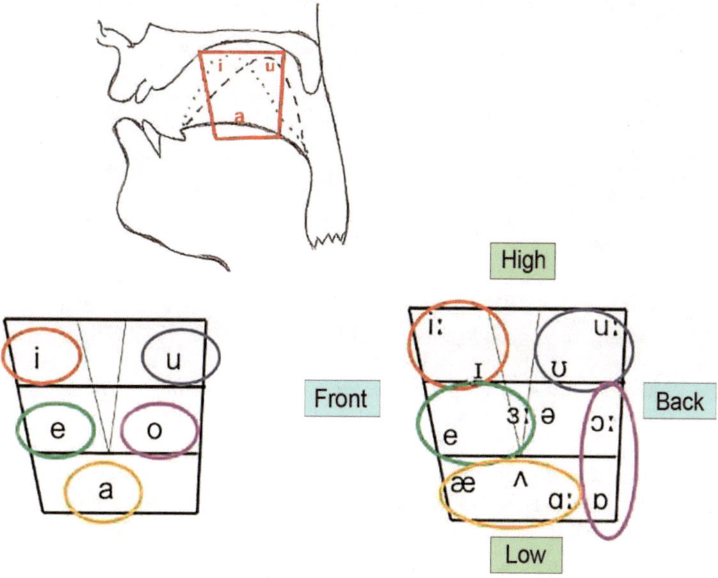

Figure 2. Different vowel systems of Spanish and English respectively. Adapted from *Teach Yourself English Phonetics* (2019), by Eva Estebas Vilaplana

The two quadrilaterals represent the positions of the tongue in the mouth, as illustrated in the picture above. For the correct production of vowels, you should contrast the location of the English and the Spanish vowels in the respective quadrilaterals to see how close or how far apart they are (figure 2). For example, the production of the English /e/ differs from Spanish as the mouth is more open (figure 3):

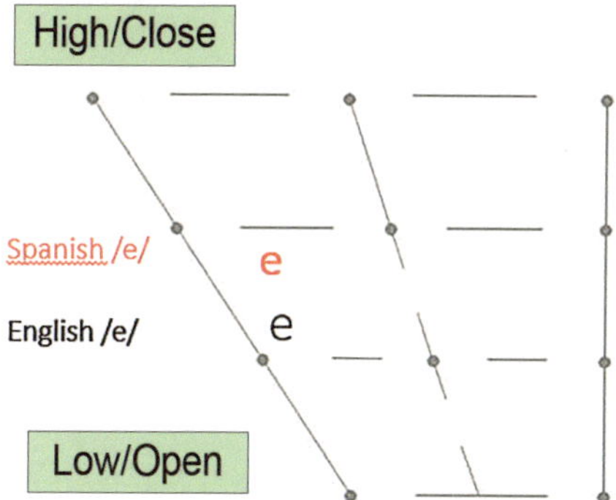

Figure 3. Comparison of Spanish and English "e" sounds

The Spanish and English vocalic systems differ not only in the number of vowels but also in their characteristics. **None of the Spanish vowels corresponds exactly with an English vowel**; you can see in the quadrilaterals of figure 2 that the vowels' articulation or the positions of the tongue are slightly different. However, Spanish speakers tend to use only the vowels they know, which replace the English sounds, as you can see in the next chart:

English vowels	Spanish vowels	English examples		Common Spanish production of the English words
/æ/		ban	/bæn/	/ban/
/ʌ/	/a/	bun	/bʌn/	/ban/
/ɑ:/		barn	/bɑn:/	/barn/
/e/	/e/	Ben	/ben/	/bern/
/ɜ:/		burn	/bɜ:n/	/ben/
/ɪ/	/i/	sin	/sɪn/	/sin/
/i:/		seen	/si:n/	/sin/
/ɒ/	/o/	con	/kɒn/	/kon/
/ɔ:/		corn	/kɔ:n/	/korn/
/ʊ/	/u/	full	/fʊl/	/ful/
/u:/		fool	/fu:l/	/ful/

Figure 4. Differences between English and Spanish vowels. Adapted from *Teach Yourself English Phonetics* (2019), by Eva Estebas Vilaplana

Note, for example, that in Spanish there is only one /a/ whereas there are three different vowels in English. **Vowels differ in quality** (are pronounced differently depending on the articulation) **as well as in quantity or length**. Thus, English /ɑ:/ can be easily differentiated from Spanish /a/ because /ɑ:/ is a longer vowel. Besides, the quality is also different because for the production of the English /ɑ:/, the tongue is at the back whereas the Spanish /a/ is more central. The difference between Spanish /a/ and English /ʌ/ and /æ/ has to do only with quality (because all of them are short). /ʌ/ is the most similar to the Spanish /a/; notice how near they are in the following quadrilateral:

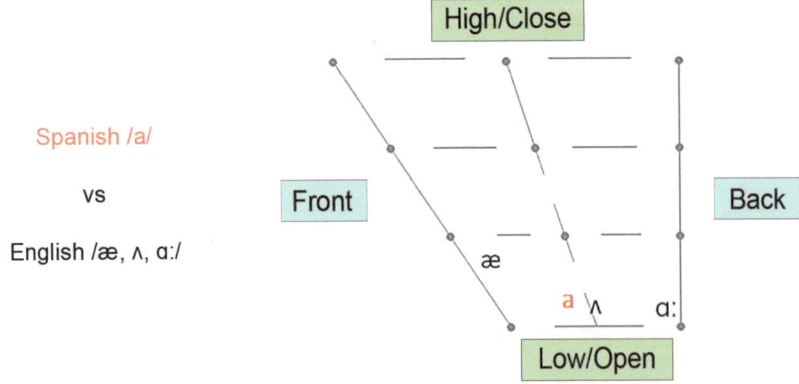

Figure 5. Comparison of Spanish and English "a" sounds

Listen to these trios of words in which the English vowels /æ, ʌ, ɑ:/ are compared. Can you hear the difference?

Figure 6. Sounds contrasts from *Timesaver Pronunciation Activities* (2005), by Bill Bowler, p. 53

In English, we can classify the vowels according to whether they are short or long. There are the 7 short vowels and 5 long vowels, and we use a colon to indicate the length, as you can see in the following chart:

VOWELS							
SHORT	/ɪ/	/ʊ/	/ɒ/	/e/	/ʌ/	æ/	/ə/
LONG	/i:/	/u:/	/ɔ:/	/ɜ:/	/ɑ:/		

It is very useful to learn and practice the contrasts between the different vowels by working with pairs which contain each sound, as well as representative pictures that can help you to remember more easily the sounds (visual cues). To make learning more meaningful and communicative, graphic organizers such as semantic-phonetic maps will also be commonly promoted. Let's look at the first example in which we can compare the pair /i:/ and /ɪ/ (/i:/ is long and /ɪ/ is short).

II.   DISCRIMINATING SOUNDS THROUGH PAIRS

Sound pair 1. SHIP OR SHEEP? Sounds /ɪ/ and /i:/

Visual cues: pictures to remember the two sounds; picture from *Fonética inglesa práctica* (2010), by Jelena Bobkina and Miriam Fernández. Graphic organizer: semantic-phonetic map of body parts containing /ɪ/

The short vowel sound /ɪ/, which is equivalent to our vowel in Spanish, normally corresponds to graphemes "**i**" or "**y**": *dish, bill, fit, ticket, city, happy, crazy, twenty.* However, remember that in English sounds may be represented by many different spellings, as in the following frequently used words: *village, pretty, women, busy, minute, business, biscuit, build.* Furthermore: /ɪ/ is also present in the **suffix of superlatives** (*biggest*), in the **endings "-age/-ege"** (*marriage, language, college*) and in the **prefixe "be-", "re-", "pre-", "de-"** (*behave, remember, prevent, depend*).

/**i:**/ is a long sound. The most usual spellings for this sound are "**ee**", "**ea**", "**ie**" and "**ei**": e.g. *tree, tea, piece, ceiling.* Watch the following video (scan QR or go to BBC_Sounds of English_Long Vowel /i:/) and pay attention to how this vowel is produced, e.g. notice how the mouth is almost closed and the lips are completely spread, as shown in figure 1. Bear in mind that using technlogy, including short videos with sounds and particularly images, "can make it easier for students to understand the mechanics of articulation" and "has been shown to help learners improve their ability to identify sounds and words" (Yoshida 2018, p. 197).

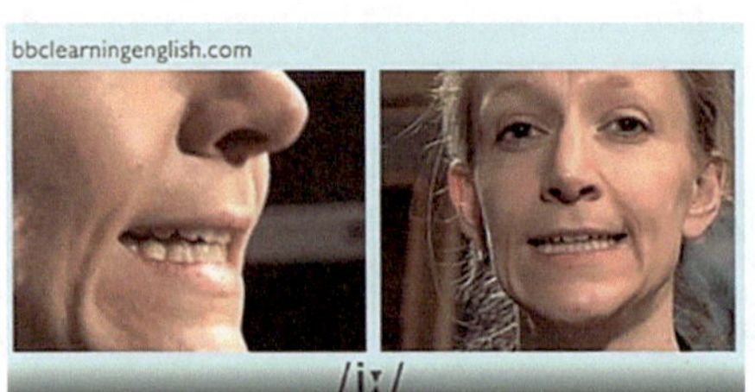

Figure 7. Illustration of the pronunciation of a given individual sound

Knowing this difference can help us distinguish easily confused words for Spanish speakers as we do not have long vowels. So, remember, when you say *I can see a sheep*, make sure you pronounce the vowel in *sheep* as long (/i:/); otherwise, you would be saying *I can see a ship*.

EXERCICES: 

1-. Semantic-Phonetic maps. Use graphic organizers to classify the following animals according to their pronunciation (a group for each of the target sounds,/ɪ, i:/):

fish, zebra, sheep, beaver, insect, pig, peacock, cheetah, iguana, chimpanzee, seal, giraffe

2-. Try to guess pronunciation based on the 'spelling rules' explained above. Place the following words in the right column according to their pronunciation:

heat, hit, leave, live, eat, it, bean, bin, feet, fit, team, tim

/ɪ/	/i:/
ship	sheep

3-. Circle the words with the same vowel sound as "beach":

4-. Change the vowel sound to /i:/ in the following words and write down the resulting new words as explained in the example: *met* becomes *meat* or *meet* when I substitute /e/ with /i: /.

check, red, bet, men, fell, bed

5-. Find the odd one out. Which word has a different vowel sound from the others?

be, still, speak, green
these, chip, fit, hip, hit
sweet, bread, policeman, people

6-. Now listen and repeat the words to get familiarized with these different sounds. Can you perceive that the vowels in the words on the right (Sound 2) are longer?

Sound 1	Sound 2
ship	sheep
bin	bean
fill	feel
pill	peel
hit	heat
slip	sleep

7-. It is much easier to perceive the different length of the vowels when you listen to the words in isolation. Now pay attention to the length difference when the words are used in sentences instead:

8-. Listen and choose the word you hear:

1. *I can't live/leave without you.*
2. *Take the lid/lead.*
3. *There is nothing to it/eat.*
4. *The sign says 'Don't slip/sleep on the floor.'*

9-. You need to be aware of the length difference of vowels when using words in natural speech. Here are some sentences to practice this. Make sure that you read the underlined words with the appropriate long vowel sound. Record yourself and compare it with the solutions given.

Tim lives at number <u>fifteen Green Street.</u>
He prepares the family <u>meals</u> in the biggest and cleanest kitchen.
Students often make <u>cheese</u> on toast because it's quick and <u>easy</u> to prepare.
I bought my <u>niece</u> some tickets to <u>see</u> her favourite film.
We have been working on it <u>since</u> three.

Sound pair 2. FULL OR FOOL? Sounds /ʊ/ and /uː/

Visual cues: pictures to remember the two sounds (*bull* and *moon*)

The short vowel sound /**u**/, normally corresponds to the grapheme "**u**": *put, full, sugar.*

/**uː**/ is a long sound. The most usual spellings for this sound are "**oo**", "**ou**", "**ue**", "**ui**", "**o**", "**u**": *food, soon, group, through, blue, true, juice, fruit, move, lose,* *rude, june.* When the spelling is "**u**" or "**ew**", this is often preceded by a /j/ sound (similar to Spanish "i"): *music, new.*

 Notice a limited number of words (*foot, took, cook, book, look, good, wood, wool*), are pronounced with /ʊ/ even if they are spelt with "oo". The same applies to the following modal verbs: *could, would* and *should.* Finally, mind the pronunciation of "*woman*" and "*wolf*". Otherwise, the general tendency is for "oo" to be pronounced /u:/.

Listen to the following pairs of words and distinguish the length difference:

Figure 8. Sound contrasts *from Timesaver Pronunciation Activities* (2005), by Bill Bowler, p. 48

EXERCICES: 

1-. Listen to these pair of sentences which only differ in one sound (one word containing either /u:/ or /ʊ/, e.g. *Luke* vs *look*). Decide in which order they are pronounced; write 1 for the first sentence you hear and 2 for the second:

Luke! It's me! ⇒ /u:/   2

Look! It's me! ⇒ /ʊ/   1

It's a blue <u>pool</u> ⇒ /u:/

It's a blue <u>pull</u> ⇒ /ʊ/

The <u>suit</u> is filthy ⇒ /u:/

The <u>soot</u> is filthy ⇒ /ʊ/

The bird <u>cooed</u> ⇒ /u:/

The bird <u>could</u> ⇒ /ʊ/

It's twenty-<u>two</u> eleven ⇒ /u:/

It's twenty <u>to</u> eleven ⇒ /ʊ/

2-. Underline the words with the sound /u:/ in the following story:

Lucy studied journalism at university in New York last fall. She had moved there for two months before summer, May and June, and then she looked for a beautiful apartment with a view. She used to go out for lunch in rooftops and try different food to amuse herself. Soon she knew that she was running out of money and she had to return to Europe. It was just too good to be true.

3-. Dictation: write down the sentences you hear by paying special attention to the words which only differ in one sound. Then record your voice to compare your production of the target sounds with the recording:

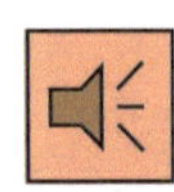 

4-. Circle the words that have /u:/ or /ʊ/ with the aid of the 'spelling rules' explained above. Then put the words in the right column:

Is it really (true?)   *The guests will arrive soon.*

You are standing on my (foot!)   *Here's your ticket, don't lose it!*

He's a good cook.   *Do you like spicy food?*

Where's my toothbrush?   *Where did you put my wallet?*

Do you push or pull to open the door?   *Could you please help me with my bags?*

/u:/	/ʊ/
true	foot

Visual cues: pictures to remember the two sounds (*clock and horse*)

- The short vowel sound /ɒ/ is pronounced with a wide, open mouth and is usually spelt **"o"**: *shop, on, comedy*. Sometimes it is also spelt **"a"** and **"au"**: *was, what, because, Australia*.

  In <u>American English</u>, this sound is pronounced differently from <u>RP English</u>. Words containing /ɒ/ are produced either with /ɑː/ or with /ɒ/ although a bit longer. Note that in the first case, apart from the different length, the vowel is also different (/ɒ/ vs /ɑː/). However, the vowels are the same in the second case, which means that some words are only distinguished by vowel length (American English /ɒ/ is longer than /ɒ/ in RP English). Listen to the following examples:

lot ⇒ /ɑː/
pot ⇒ /ɑː/
watch ⇒ /ɑː/
holiday ⇒ /ɑː/

lost ⇒ longer /ɒ/
boss ⇒ longer /ɒ/
dog ⇒ longer /ɒ/
gone ⇒ longer /ɒ/

- /ɔː/ is a long sound, closer than /ɒ/ in terms of quality and pronounced with rounded lips. It has many different spellings, **"or", "oor", "ore", "our" "ough", "augh", "au", "ar", "al", "aw"**: *horse, born, door, floor, more, before, four, thought, bought, , taught, daughter, author, autumn, war, warm, ball, wall, talk, saw, law*.

  In <u>American English</u>, /ɔː/ only occurs when followed by an /r/, as in *war*. Otherwise, it is replaced by that longer /ɒ/ mentioned above, which is a vowel more open than /ɔː/. Compare the pronunciation of the following words in RP and AE respectively: *law, all, paw*.

EXERCICES: 

1-. Listen to the following pairs of sentences which only differ in one sound (one word containing either /ɒ/ or /ɔː/, e.g. *Don* vs *Dawn*) and decide in which order they are pronounced; write 1 for the first sentence you hear and 2 for the second.

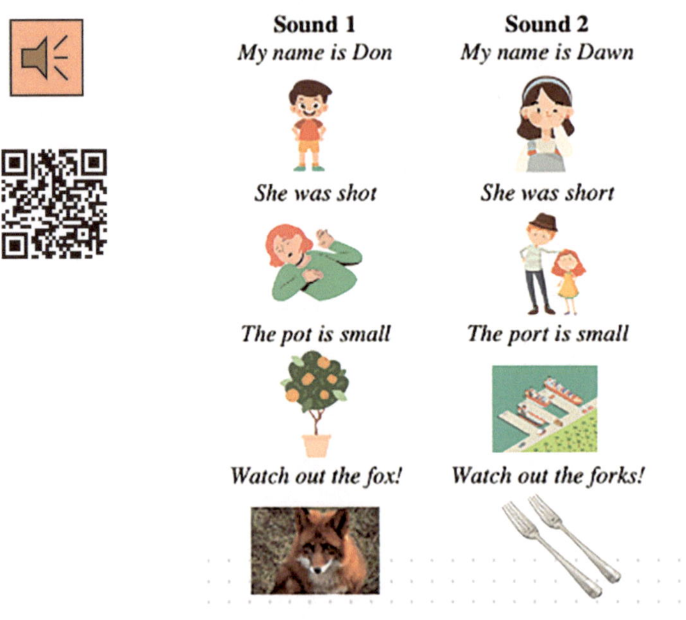

2-. Tick the word that you hear in the sentences:

1. I don't like those _______ .	spots	☐	sports	☐
2. This _______ is empty.	pot	☐	port	☐
3. There's a large _______ over there.	cod	☐	cord	☐
4. The police officer was _______ .	shot	☐	short	☐
5. Don't pick up that unknown _______ .	collar	☐	caller	☐
6. The burglar was _______ .	cot	☐	caught	☐

3-. Listen to the following words and decide whether they are pronounced with American English or RP English:

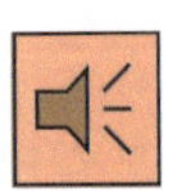 

fog	RP	*cough*	
lodge		*cost*	
not		*moth*	
cod		*cross*	
odd		*cloth*	

Sound pair 4. HEAD OR HEARD? Sounds /e/ and /ɜ:/

Visual cues: pictures to remember the two sounds (*hen* and *bird*)

The short vowel sound /**e**/ is normally spelt "**e**", but also "**ea**", "**ai**", "**ay**", "**ie**", "**a**", "**u**": *dress, bed, bread, head, said, again, says, friend, any, bury.*

/**ɜ:**/ is a long vowel and is spelt "**er**", "**ear**", "**ir**", "**or**", "**ur**", "**our**": *her, perfect, early, heard, bird, first, work, world, burn, chu ch, journey, courtesy.*

EXERCICES: 

1-. You will hear a set of words from the box. If you hear the same word twice, write S (same). If you hear two different words, write D (different): e.g. 1. *head/heard:* D.

peck/perk; nest/nursed; ten/turn; bed/bird; went/weren't; end/earned

2.   5.

3.   6.

4.   7.

2-. Listen and circle the word you hear: e.g. *bed/*bird

1. *ten/turn*   3. *west/worst*

2. *bent/ burnt*   4. *lend/learned*

3-. Listen and choose the word that you hear:

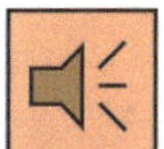

1. He's got a big bed/bird at home.
2. Betty/Bertie phoned you.
3. She lends/learns lots of things.
4. The sign says 'ten/turn'.
5. It's the west/worst wind.

Sound pair 5. CAT OR CUT? Sounds /æ/ and /ʌ/

Visual cues: pictures to remember the two sounds (c*a*t and d*u*ck)

/æ/ is a short sound which is pronounced with a wide open mouth, as shown in the picture below. The most common spelling is "**a**": *cat, lamp, hand, marry, ran, back, map, apple.* Scan QR to hear how to pronounce /æ/:

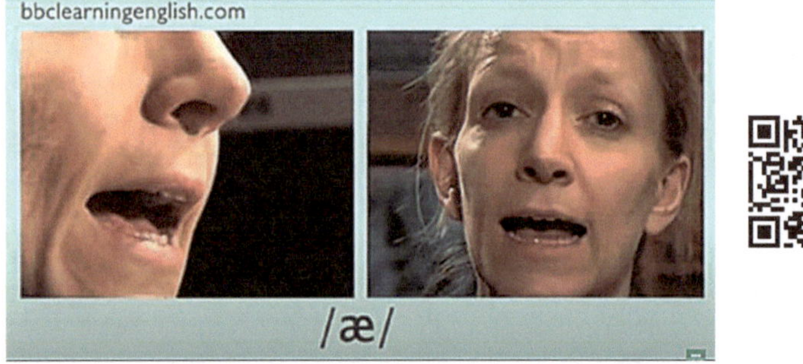

Figure 9. Illustration of the pronunciation of a given individual sound

- /ʌ/ is also short and is very similar to the Spanish /a/. It is usually spelt "**u**", but other common spellings include "**o**", "**ou**", "**oe**": *cut, sun, bus, luck, study, come, son, love, worry, mother, touch, young, does.*

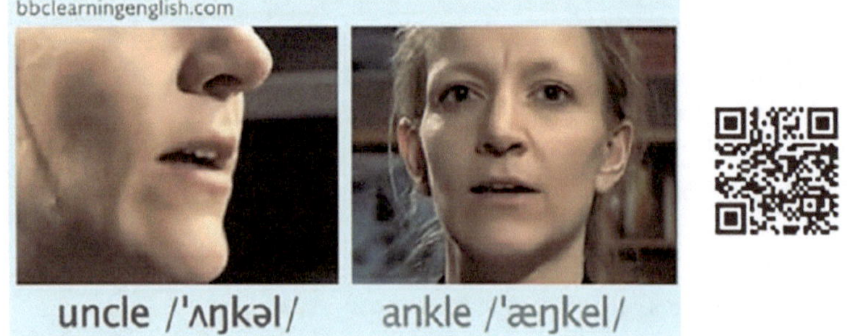

Figure 10. Articulation of /ʌ/ and comparison with the sound /æ/

EXERCICES: 

1-. Try to guess pronunciation based on the 'spelling rules' explained above. Place the following words in the right column according to their pronunciation:

bag, country, plan, jam, number, colour, husband, bank, traffic, butter

/æ/	/ʌ/
bag	country

2-. Change the vowel sound to /ʌ/ in the following words and write down the resulting new words as explained in the example: ***ankle*** becomes ***uncle*** when I substitute /æ/ with /ʌ /:

cap, hat, bag, mad, hang, ran, cat, bat, began, sang, track, match, fan, mad, banker, rash, flatter, baddie, crash, bang, bank, rang, flash, cab, dad, fanned, rag

3-. Tick the word that you hear in the sentences:

	track ☐	truck ☐
1. What a big __________!		
2. I love this _______ .	hat ☐	hut ☐
3. Take care of the__________________.	cap ☐	cup ☐
4. That's a bad _______ .	cat ☐	cut ☐
5. I _______ my coat on the door.	hang ☐	hung ☐
6. They _______ quickly.	ran ☐	run ☐

4-. Semantic-Phonetic maps. Use graphic organizers to classify the following vegetables according to their pronunciation (a group for each of the target sounds, /æ/ and /ʌ/):

salad, mushroom, eggplant, cabbage, carrot, pumpkin, cucumber, yam, asparagus

5-. Find the odd one out. Which word has a different vowel sound from the others?

month, January, Monday, Sunday
mother, brother, husband, father
ran, study, come, touch
luck, business, fun, duck
just, one, glad, done
word, money, above, double
oven, flood, blood, push
London, Russia, common, love

Sound pair 6. HAT OR HEART? Sounds /æ/ and /ɑː/

Visual cues: pictures to remember the two sounds (*ba*t and *calf*)

/æ/ is a short vowel and is generally spelt "**a**": *cat, lamp, hand, marry, ran, back, map, apple.*

/**ɑː**/ is long and more open in terms of quality. It is typically spelt "**a**" or "**ar**", but also "**an**", "**al**", "**au**" and "**ear**": *ask, bath, car, march, dance, plant, calm, half, laugh, aunt, heart.*

In <u>American English</u>, some words containing /ɑː/ are produced with /æ/. This occurs when there is no /l/ or /r/ after the vowel. Listen to the following examples of words pronounced in RP English and AE respectively (Estebas-Vilaplana 2009): e.g., *fast, last, bath, laugh, glass, chance.*

EXERCICES: 

1-. Try to guess pronunciation based on the 'spelling rules' explained above. Place the following words in the right column according to their pronunciation:

garden, cash, talk, jacket, carry, factory, camera, class, fast, father

/æ/	/ɑː/
cash	artist

2-. Decide which is the correct vowel (/æ, ʌ, ɑː/) in the following words:

lark: /ɑː/	*lack:*	*luck:*
bad:	*bard:*	*bud:*
match:	*much:*	*march:*
cart:	*cut:*	*cat:*
cup:	*carp:*	*cap:*
hut:	*hat:*	*heart:*

3-. Find a route from the start to the end. Moves can be horizontal, vertical or diagonal but you may pass a square only if the /ɑ:/ sound in it is pronounced.

START

dark	drunk	watch	fan	can
smart	cat	starts	sunk	rabbit
class	half	can't	mother	staff
ham	jam	calm	father	dance
draw	bag	dare	man	card

END

4-. Circle the word that you hear (note that here you also have to compare the three vowels sounds previously explained /æ, ʌ, ɑ:/):

1. *hat/hut/heart*

2. *cat/cut/cart*

3. *cap/cup/carp*

4. *ban/bun/barn*

5. *bad/bud/bard*

6. *back/buck/bark*

THE SCHWA: Sound /ə/

Visual cues: pictures to remember the two sounds (*astonomer, teacher, driver, doctor*)

The schwa, /ə/, is a short vowel and it only appears in **unstressed syllables.**[1] This sound poses general problems for Spanish speakers, even those at an advanced level of English (Calvo-Brenzies 2013, p. 47). Since this sound does not exist in Spanish, most students tend to use the Spanish vowels they know and guide their pronunciation according to the spelling of a given word. For example , in *banana*, they will use the Spanish /a/ in all unstressed syllables (/*banana*/), in *pencil* they will use the /i/ (pencil) and in *police*, the /o/ (/police/). Listen to these words (from Estebas-Vilaplana 2009) which are very similar in English and Spanish in terms of spelling and stress but differ in their pronunciation (note how all the unstressed syllables have the schwa): *Amanda, camera, Marina, Serena, Bonanza.*

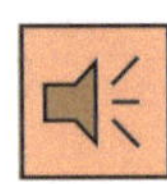 

To pronounce it correctly, try to put your mouth neutral or slightly opened and say *ehhhh* (as when you doubt). This sound requires very little effort, it is scarcely audible, so do not move any other articulator apart from opening your mouth. To better imitate the sound, you can watch the following video accompanied by a further explanation of how to articulate schwa:

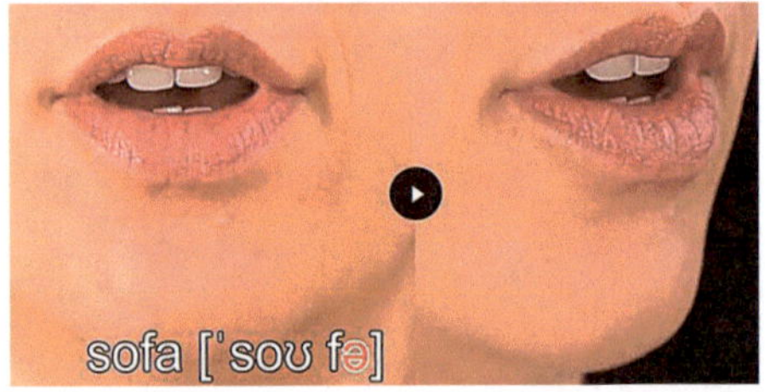

"How to Pronounce the Schwa", from https://rachelsenglish.com/

"It's possible to make this sound on its own with just the slightest jaw drop. But in actual words, you will likely see a bit more jaw drop, like here, on the word 'sofa'. Lips relaxed, cheeks relaxed, tongue forward and relaxed."

In terms of spelling, **all five vowel letters can represent this sound**: *alone, broken, impossible, produce, suspect.* Here you have some more examples:

- Initial position: *alone, appear, occur, official, oppose, balloon, supply, suggest.*

- Mid position: *Canada, certainly, customer, analysis.*

- Final position: *comma, letter, soldier, lasagne.*

Furthermore, it can be spelt as a combination of two vowel letters: *nation, glamorous.*

---

[1] Stressed syllables are the ones carrying the prominence in a word or what we call accentuation in Spanish; they are easily recognized as being louder and longer than unstressed syllables. A stressed syllable is indicated with the symbol /'/, e.g., in *better*, the stressed syllable is the first one and the unstressed syllable has got the weak vowel schwa: /'betə/. See unit 4 for more information about Stress.

Very typically, it also corresponds to the combination of a vowel letter (or two vowel letters) followed by "r": *father, colour*.

Finally, it occurs in many **professions** and nouns ending in "er" and "or" (e.g. *teacher, photographer, donor, doctor*), as shown in the visual cues, and most **suffixes,** such as "ous", "lous", "eous", "able", "ure" and "ion", among others. It is common to hear Spanish speakers pronounce these suffixes according to the spelling rather than with simply a schwa. Using a dictionary, check the following examples and remember to make this easy rule of pronunciation extensible to all the words you know in English with similar endings: *jealous, obvious, marvelous, simultaneous, fashionable, reasonable, culture, nature, manufacture, devotion, organization.*

Although Spanish does not have the schwa, it is **the most frequent sound in English,** which appears in almost every word with more than two syllables. Besides, it is very important for the correct production of stress and rhythm in English.

Indeed, this sound is essential for understanding and imitating **natural spoken English** as it regularly appears in all the **grammar words** (see a more detailed explanation about connected speech and the so-called weak forms in the last unit). Listen to these audios from BBC Learning English in which you can appreciate how the schwa typically appears in unstressed syllables and grammar words (e.g. prepositions, pronouns, and articles):

*This present is **f**or my broth**er**. It's **a** book **a**bout **a** boy wiz**ar**d. To s**ur**vive the cold weath**er** you have t**o** make thor**ough** preparati**o**ns.*

BE AWARE... and CHECK! It is very important to apply your phonetics knowledge whenever you use English in spontaneous conversation. An excellent way to do so is to track your pronunciation of sounds such as the schwa. For example, you can start recording yourself reading short passages of texts or reciting clips from films and then check whether you pronounced the schwa in all necessary words. Later on, whenever you speak in English you should ask yourself "Have I pronounced that word with the schwa?" or "Am I pronouncing grammar words with the schwa?".

EXERCICES: 

1-. Look at these phrases or sentences and underline the vowels sounds that are pronounced with a schwa.

*I come from London
The brother was asleep
The restaurant was open
The doctor's assistant
She answered the telephone
A difficult question*

2-. Listen and circle the word you hear (Hancock 2012):

teacher's (er=/ə/ vs *teaches* (e=/ɪ/)
officer's (er=/ə/) vs *office's* (e=/ɪ/)
woman /ˈwʊmən/ vs *women* (/ˈwɪmɪn/)

Where's Kate's dress/address?
Take that away/way.
The German teacher's/teaches English.
What a nice driver/drive!
The officer's/office's here.
What time did the woman/women arrive?
The drivers sleep/driver's asleep in the van.

3-. Look at these words and decide where the schwa sound occurs (remember it can only appear in unstressed syllables):

*e.g. profess**or***	*remember*
tomorrow	*important*
summer	*readable*
protect	*about*
wonderful	*theatre*
emotion	*treasure*

4-. Look at these sentences and decide where the schwa sound occurs (remember that it appears in unstressed syllables and grammar words):

1. *It's a present for you.*
2. *It takes a long time to get there.*
3. *Would you like a cup of tea?*
4. *What are you doing tonight?*
5. *What time will you arrive at the station?*
6. *I have been studying English for 5 years.*
7. *The city centre is closed for a demonstration.*
8. *The airport is rather far from here.*
9. *She works as a teacher and as a counselour for the government.*
10. *We need some more help from the local autorities.*

Now read aloud the sentences by paying special attention to the presence of shwa in grammar words (weak forms). Here is a useful video lesson to help you and for extra practice:

5-. Try to pronounce the schwa in these sentences. The transcription of the schwa sound is provided in the words on the right to help you (note how it appears in grammar words and unstressed syllables). Record your voice to compare your production with that of the recording:

a credible story of fiction	ə crediblə story əf fictən
a book about life and love	ə book əbout life ənd love
a bottle of water	ə bottlə əf watər
a photograph of my sister	ə photəgraph əf my sistər
a married couple and the children	ə married couplə ənd thə childrən
a picture is worth a thousand words	ə pictə is worth ə thousənd words
an apple a day keeps the doctor away	ən applə ə day keeps thə doctə əway

6.- Keep practicing and realizing how often the schwa appears by reading this story. Again, the transcription of the target sound has been provided to help you. Record your voice and then listen to your own production t o check whether yo u pronounced properly /ə/ in all the necessary words:

My parənts met ət Cəlumbiə University in 1964. They werən't studənts, no one in their immediəte families həd evər gone tə college.

My mothər wəs ə secrətəry in thə admissionəns office; my fathər wəs ə clerk in əccounting. They worked in thə same building, passing each othər in the halls, riding thə elevatər təgethər, sərrounded by othər clericəl ənd service workərs, prəfessərs ənd studənts, stealing glances ət each othər.

My mothər wəs seventeen years old. I həve ə photəgraph əf hər frə m that time. She wəs beautifəl, exotic in thə white, uppər-class world in which she ənd my fathər found thəmselves ənd each othər. She had ambitən, wanted tə be something, anything. Wanted most əf all, despərətely, tə get out əf Harləm.

My fathər həd nevər seen anything like hər. My fathər wəs twenty. His whole world həd been thə few blocks əf his Bronx neighbərhood, ə predominəntly Italiən world.

Excerpt adapted from *The Skin between us: A Memoir of Racem Beauty and Belonging* (2006),
by Kym Ragusa

You can use any of these recording programs that allow students to record themselves speaking, some of which provide you also with the transcription of your speech: Recorder Pro, Dragon Dictate, Audacity, Wave Pad. For additional practice with other texts and scripts, visit Voicetube, which offers plenty of authentic videoclips of different length and levels.

2. CONSONANTS

[TESTING YOUR] PRELIMINARY KNOWLEDGE

Here are some questions to reflect on some basic notions of English pronunciation:
1. How many consonants are there in English? Are they the same than in Spanish?
2. Write down the words associated to the pictures below.
3. Can you establish any relationship between the letters/spelling of the words (graphemes) and the phonetic symbols?

Figure 0. English consonants (phonetic symbols)

I.   DIFFERENCES BETWEEN THE ENGLISH AND SPANISH CONSONANT SYSTEMS

Place of articulation							
bilabial	labio-dental	dental	alveolar	palate-alveolar	palatal	velar	glottal
p b			t d			k g	
				tʃ dʒ			
	f v	θ ð	s z	ʃ ʒ			h
m			n			ŋ	
			l				
w				r	j	w	

Figure 1. Classification of the English consonants according to their Place of articulation, which refers to the <u>Speech organs</u> involved in their pronunciation. Adapted from *How to Teach Pronunciation* (2000), by Gerald Kelly. See also Annex 3 for a helpful visual illustration

[HOW TO AVOID] COMMON MISTAKES

◊ **MIND THE DIFFERENT CONSONANT**

Spanish **/r/** vs English **/r/**; Spanish **/j/** vs English **/j/**

✖ Common mistake:

red:   

✔ Correct pronunciation

red:

☞ Explanation: even if they are transcribed the same (/r/), Spanish *r* sounds differently from English as their place of articulation is also different. Whereas in Spanish the tip of the tongue is touching the alveolar ridge (the point behind your upper teeth: see Annex 3), for the production of English /r/, you should curl back the tongue tip towards the alveolar ridge (without touching it!) and round your lips. Listen:

✖ Common mistake

yesterday:  

✔ Correct pronunciation

yesterday:  

☞ Explanation: in English there are a few consonant sounds (9 exactly!) that do not exist in Spanish such as /j/, which Spanish speakers typically confuse with /j/ (as in the words *llevar* or *yo*) but actually sounds more similarly to the Spanish /i/ vowel sound.

◊ **MIND THE VOICING DIFFERENCE**

Spanish **/s/** vs English **/z/**

✖ Common mistake

ice/eyes:  

✔ Correct pronunciation:

ice/eyes: 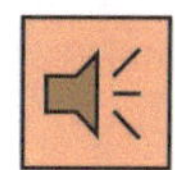 

☞ Explanation: Spanish speakers fail to pronounce the 'buzzing' sound in the word *zoo* as they do not know that in English some sounds are voiced, which refers to the vibration of the vocal cords during speech production.

In this unit, you will learn some consonant sounds that do not exist in Spanish and one important characteristic of English pronunciation: the difference between voiceless and voiced consonants.

This will improve your understanding and pronunciation. More importantly, you will avoid very common misunderstandings because some Spanish speakers generally lack knowledge about the phonemes of the English system, which obviously differ from Spanish. Just the same as with the vowels, there are a few differences to learn when it comes to the consonant sounds.

The following sets of pairs will help you to learn the consonant sounds in English and how to avoid frequent mistakes. In addition, the accompanying visual cues will help you to remember the most important consonants which either do not exist in Spanish or are pronounced differently.

II.   DISCRIMINATING SOUNDS THROUGH PAIRS

Sound pair 1. SEA OR SHE? Sounds /s/ and /ʃ/

sea shells on the sea shore

Visual cue: *sea shells on the sea shore*

- /s/ is the same sound as the Spanish one in the word *sol*. It is usually spelt "**s**", "**ss**", "**c**" and sometimes "**sc**": *sit, bus, class, glass, city, place, science, scissors.*

- /ʃ/ appears at the beginning of words such as *show, shop, sugar*. This sound is similar to the sound we make when we want children to be quiet (*shhhhh*). The most common spelling is "**sh**", but it can be spelt in many other ways: "**s**" (*sure*), "**c**" (*ocean*), "**ch**" (*machine*), "**ci**" (*special*), "**ti**" (*international*).

    *Although this sound is present in some Catalan, Andalusian or Galician words, it is not part of the Spanish standard pronunciation system and therefore Spanish speakers do not use it in English. Instead, they tend to use /s/ in words where they should be using /ʃ/. As a result, one frequent mistake is to say /si:/ (that is, the noun *sea*) rather than /ʃi:/ (the pronoun *she*).

Look at the following examples in which by only changing one sound (using /s/ instead of /ʃ/), the meaning is also completely different.

sea ≠ she   *so ≠ show*
seat ≠ sheet   *fist ≠ fished*
sock ≠ shock   *sign ≠ shine*
save ≠ shave   *same ≠ shame*
seal ≠ she'll   *sip ≠ ship*

EXERCICES: 

1-. You will hear two words from the box. If you hear the same word twice, write S (same). If you hear two different words, write D (different): e.g. 1. *seat/sheet*: S.

sea/she; so/show; same/shame; self/shelf; fist/fished; sell/shell

 2.   3.

 4.   5.

6.   7.

2-. Listen and choose the word you hear:

1. *so/show*   4. *save/shave*
2. *seat/sheet*   5. *sign/shine*
3. *suit/shoot*   6. *fist/fished*

Sound pair 2. SUE OR ZOO? Sounds /s/ and /z/

Visual cue: *the<u>se</u> ja<u>zz</u> mu<u>s</u>ician<u>s</u>*

- /s/ is the same sound as the Spanish one in the word *sol*. It is usually spelt "**s**", "**ss**", "**c**" and sometimes "**sc**": *sit, bus, class, glass, city, place, science, scissors*.

- /**z**/ is the voiced counterpart of /s/. To pronounce /z/, put your hands in your vocal cords and make sure you feel the **vibration**. Note that /s/ sounds like the noise of a snake whereas /z/ sounds like a bee. Apart from feeling the vibration of the vocal cords when pronouncing /z/, the voiced consonant lengthens the duration of the preceding vowel. For example, the vowel in *peas* (with /z/) is longer than in *piece (*with /s/).

There are many words which contain this sound in English, as you can see in the picture above (count how many /z/ sounds there are in the sentence *A lazy zebra called Desmond is dozing at the zoo. He feels flies buzzing round his eyes, ears and nose*).

The most common spellings are "**z**" and "**zz**": *zero, size, jazz, buzz*. It is also a characteristic sound of the ending or **morpheme "-s"** (*gives, sisters*)[1], and of **intervocalic "s"** (between two vowels: *easy, rose*). Less frequently, it can be spelt "**ss**", as in *scissors*.

*As this consonant does not exist in Spanish, the words containing /z/ are pronounced with /s/. This will cause misunderstandings since, for example, *Sue* and *zoo* will be pronounced in the same way. Look at the following examples in which by only changing one sound (using /s/ instead of /z/), the meaning is also completely different:

abuse (n.) ≠ abuse (v.)[2]   *rice ≠ rise*
advice ≠ advise   *ice ≠ eyes*
place ≠ plays   *tense ≠ tens*
race ≠ raise   *face ≠ phase*
Bruce ≠ brews   *pace ≠ pays*

EXERCICES: 

1-. Listen and choose the word you hear:

place/plays   *niece/knees*   *pace/pays*

Sue/zoo   *piece/peas*   *ice/eyes*

---

[1] See Unit 3, about morphemic rules.

[2] Note how **pronunciation is linked to grammar**: nouns/adjectives are pronounced with /s/ and distinguished from verbs, which are pronounced with /z/. More examples: *use* (/ju:s/ as a noun) vs *use* (/ju:z/ as a verb); *house* (/haus/as a noun) vs *house* (/hauz/ as a verb); *close* (/kl;us/ as an adjective) vs *close* (/kl;uz/ as a verb).

2-. Look at the underlined words (from Hancock 2012, p. 17) and identify the words which contain the consonant /s/ and those which contain /z/ (pay attention to the category: noun, verb or adjective; see note 2). Then listen and repeat.

You can have my tent. It's no <u>use</u> /s/ to me. I never <u>use</u>/z/ it.
I'm not going to <u>advise</u> you. You never take my <u>advice</u>.
Your tooth is <u>loose</u>. You'll <u>lose</u> it if you're not careful.
The shop's very <u>close</u> to home, and it doesn't <u>close</u> till late.
I can't <u>excuse</u> people who drop litter. There's no <u>excuse</u> for it.

3-. Listen and circle the word you hear (Hancok 2012, p. 17):

Price or prize? /s/ and /z/	*It's a good <u>price/prize</u>.*
He sat or he's at? /s/ and /z/	*I don't know where <u>he sat/he's at</u>.*
Suit or shoot? /s/ and /z/	*They didn't <u>suit/shoot</u> him.*
Saved or shaved? /s/ and /ʃ/	*I''ve <u>saved/shaved</u> a lot in he past few days!*

Sound pair 3. CHEAP OR JEEP? Sounds /tʃ/ and /dʒ/

a large orange jacket
Visual cue: *a large orange <u>j</u>acket*

/tʃ/ is the same sound as the Spanish one at the beginning of the words *chocolate* or *chorizo*. The most common spellings in English are "**ch**" and "**tch**", as in *church* and *watch*. The ending "**-ture**", in well-known words such as *nature, culture* or *furniture*, also has this sound.

/dʒ/ is the voiced counterpart of /tʃ/, which appears in the words *James, joke, jeep*, and is the same sound as the Spanish /j/ in the words *yo* and *mayo* but with more emphasis. The most common spellings are "**g**", "**j**", "**ge**", "**dg**": *gym, june, age, badge*.

Look at the following examples in which by only changing one sound (using /tʃ/ instead of /dʒ/), the meaning is completely different:

chin ≠ gin   choke ≠ joke
chest ≠ jest   rich ≠ ridge

EXERCICES: 

1-. Place the following words in the right column according to their pronunciation (with the aid of the 'spelling rules' explained above):

lounge, bridge; chair; large; chicken; cheap; juice; Dutch; language; chips; orange; cheese; dangerous

/tʃ/	/dʒ/
teacher	

2-. Find the odd one out: Which word has a different vowel sound from the others?

larger	*generally*	*guess*	*fridge*
village	*get*	*Germany*	*page*
coach	*check*	*Christmas*	*temperature*
June	*vegetable*	*give*	*cabbage*
stattion	*Russian*	*picture*	*information*

3-. Read this text about Dressage and underline the words containung /tʃ/ and /dʒ/:

International dressage competition is set to return to the gorgeous 75 hectare estate of Haras de Jardy, located near Versailles palace in the quiet, green outskirts of Paris. The show will feature a full programme with young horses tests and classes for pony, children, junior, young and riders up to Grand Prix.

Priding itself on history and experience in the management of international show jumping and eventing competitions as well as national dressage shows, Jardy successfully staged its first performance in 2022.

Set in tropical temperatures, the 2022 Jardy brought together a huge group of riders from nations across the world who enjoyed high quality competition in the most beautiful surrounding, celebrating French lifestyle and cuisine on site at the Orangerie restaurant, as well as having the option for dinners in the wonderful town of Versailles.

Jardy is a horse paradise with Norman style buildings, spacious arenas, and plenty of green park and paddocks surrounding the property.

Source: adapted from "International Dressage Returns to Jardy" (eurodressage.com)

a pleasurable massage

Visual cue: *a pleasurable massage*

- As explained previously, /ʃ/ appears at the beginning of words such as *show, shop, sugar* and the most common spelling is **"sh"**, but it can be spelt in many other ways: **"s"** (*sure*), **"c"** (*ocean*), **"ch"** (*machine*), **"ci"** (*special*), **"ti"** (*international*).

- /ʒ/ is the voiced equivalent of /ʃ/ and appears in words such as *pleasure* or *television*. It is usually spelt **"si"** (*Asia, conclusion*) but there are other spellings: **"g"** (genre), **"-ge"** (words from French origin e.g. *beige, massage*) and **"s, ss, z + u"** (*measure, usually*).

*This sound is not used in standard Spanish and is the voiced equivalent of the consonant /ʃ/ in English. It is therefore important not to confuse it either with /ʃ/ or even /s/, and try to make the effort to pronounce it correctly. As useful analogies you can emulate, try to produce the same sound of the French word *rouge* or the Argentinian *llover*.

EXERCICES 

1-. Write the spelling of the words corresponding to the following transcriptions and put them in the correct column:

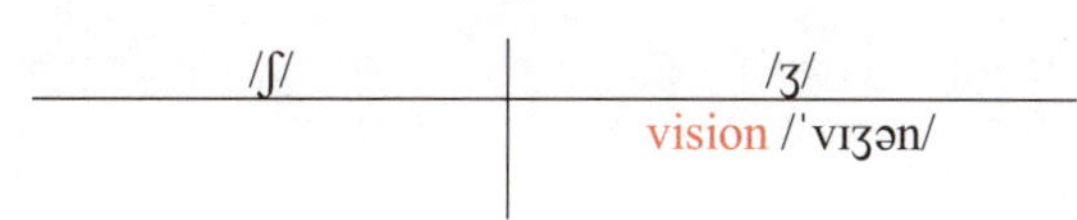

/ˈvɪʒən/; /ˈʃʊgə/; /əˈluːʒən/; /məˈʃiːn//ˈpærəʃuːt/; /dɪˈvɪʒən/ /brʌʃ/; /ˈmeʒə/; /ˈkæʒuəl/; /ˈleʒə/

/ʃ/	/ʒ/
	vision /ˈvɪʒən/

2-. First put these words into the correct column. Then record yourself saying the words and listen to your recording again in a few days. Can you clearly hear the difference between the two sounds you pronounced?

Spanish; Russia; pleasure; shake; measure; fashion; shirt; casual; revision; wash; nation; cash; ocean

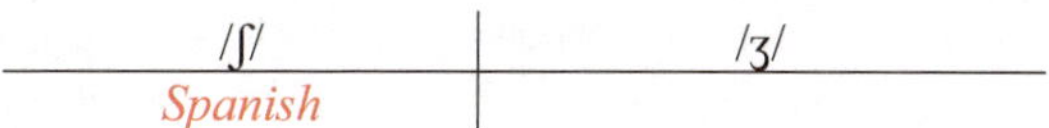

/ʃ/	/ʒ/
Spanish	

3-. Listen to the following words and decide whether they contain /ʃ/ or /ʒ/:

	/ʃ/	/ʒ/
fish	X	
patient		
profession		
ambition		
exposure		
beige		
unusual		
measure		
devotion		
anxious		
illusion		

4-. In the text above, the equestrian discipline "dressage" is pronounced with /ʒ/. Find other words with the sound /ʃ/.

Sound pair 5. LEAF OR LEAVE? Sounds /f/ and /v/

an adventorous van driver

Visual cue: an *adventorous van driver*

- There is no difference between the English and Spanish **/f/** (present in the English words *fine* or *four* and in the Spanish *faro* or *feria*).

- However, some Spanish speakers do not know that the consonant **/v/** in English is not equivalent to the Spanish sound of *vino*. In Spanish, /v/ is pronounced as the consonant /b/; this means that the words *vaso* and *barro* have the same initial consonants. In English /b/ is definitely different from /v/ as the first is a bilabial consonant (you pronounce it by putting together both of your lips) whereas the second is labiodental (here your upper teeth touch your lower lip: see Annex 3).

  Look at the following examples in which by only changing one sound (using /b/ instead of /v/), the meaning is completely different:

bury ≠ very	bet ≠ vet	beer ≠ veer	berry ≠ very	best ≠ vest
bow ≠ vow	ban ≠ van	boat ≠ vote	serb ≠ serve	bend ≠ vent

  In English, the main difference between /f/ (spelt **"f"**, **"ff"**, **"ph"**) and /v/ (spelt **"v"**) is that the first consonant is voiceless and the second one is voiced. Apart from feeling the vibration of the vocal cords when pronouncing /v/, this voiced consonant lengthens the duration of the preceding vowel. In other words, the vowel in *leave* is longer than in *leaf.*

EXERCICES:

1-. Listen to the following minimal pairs words containing /b/and /v/ and choose the word that is pronounced:

bet √	*vet*
best	*vest*
bury	*very*
by	*vie*
bow	*vow*
boat	*vote*
bowel	*vowel*
bent	*vent*
ban	*van*

2-. Listen to the minimal pairs containing /f/ and /v/ and select in which order they are pronounced; write 1 for the first word you hear and 2 for the second:

proof	1	*focal*		*half*	
prove	2	*vocal*		*halve*	
fine		*surf*			
vine		*serve*			
grief		*staff*			
grieve		*starve*			
safe		*leaf*			
save		*leave*			

Sound pair 6. THREE OR THIS? Sounds /θ/ and /ð/

how's the weather there?

Visual cue: *how's <u>the</u> <u>weather</u> <u>there</u>?*

- /θ/ is a dental sound (your tongue touches your upper teeth: See Annex 3) and corresponds to the same consonant sound that appears at the beginning of the Spanish words *zapato* or *cerilla*. The most common spelling in English is "**th**": *think, theatre, author, method, death, both.*

- /ð/ is the voiced counterpart and is the sound at the beginning of the English words *they* or *that*. The most common spelling is also "**th**": *this, then, although, breathe, brother, clothes.*

  *A frequent mistake is to confuse this sound with the Spanish /d/, which is an alveolar sound (your tongue touches your alveolar ridge, which is behind your upper teeth: See Annex 3). Therefore be careful not to pronounce *day* when you mean *they*; in other words, make sure that the tip of your tongue touches your upper teeth!

EXERCICES: 

1-. Transcribe the following words and put them in the correct column:

athletic; fourth; although; ethics; clothes; method; author; mouth

/θ/	/ð/
athletic /æθˈletɪk/	

You can use the website Photransedit (http://www.photransedit.com/online/typeipa.aspx) if you want to access the phonetic symbols/keyboard from your computer and later paste your answer in a word document.

2-. Identify the sounds /θ/ and /ð/ in the different words of these sentences. Then classify them in the appropriate column.

What are you thinking about?   *Clean all that rubbish thrown over there.*
I would like another coffee, please   *My 'teeth' are hurting.*
I am not very good at maths.   *Today is the fourth of July.*
I'm looking for the bathroom, please.   *These clothes belong to my mother.*

/θ/	/ð/
thinking	

3-. Listen first to the following pairs of words which only differ in one sound (one word containing either /d/ or /ð/, e.g. *day* vs *they*). Then decide in which order they are pronounced; write 1 for the first word you hear and 2 for the second:

Sound 1	Sound 2
day	*they*
Dan	*than*
dare	*there*
sudden	*southern*
breed	*breathe*
dough	*though*
load	*loathe*

4-. Semantic-Phonetic maps. Use any graphic organizer of your choice to group different words belonging to a similar category and containing the given sound:

 - Body parts (θ):
 - Time/Canlendar (θ):
 - Proper names (θ):
 - Family/Kinship (ð):
 - Pronouns (ð):

Sound pair 7. YALE OR JAIL? Sounds /j/ and /dʒ/

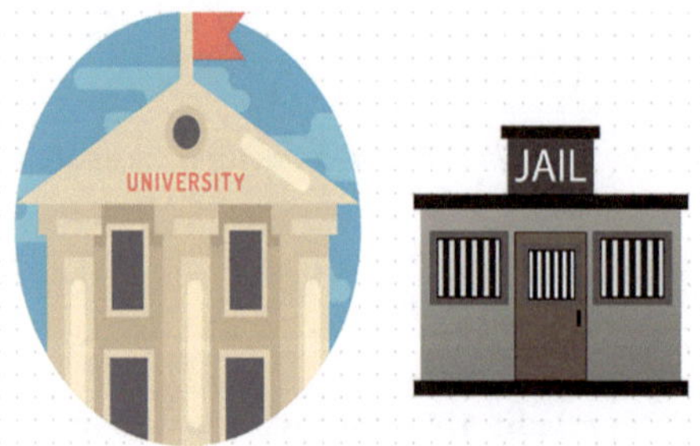

Are you going to Yale or to jail?

- **/j/** is a consonant which appears in the words *yes, yellow, usually* or *university*. It is also called a semivowel as it is similar in quality to the vowel /i/. However, sometimes it is pronounced as /ʤ/, which is a mistake. This is due to the wrong assumption that a "y" in the spelling is pronounced as the Spanish /j/ in the word *ya,* which is more or less the equivalent of /ʤ/ in English (the sound in the words *gym* or *june*).

  Therefore, remember that grapheme **"y"** in English corresponds to semivowel /j/ and not /ʤ/ (or Spanish /j/). Some words can be easily confused if you do not pay enough attention to this difference; for example, if you say *jail* when you meant *Yale* or *jet* instead of *yet*. Look at a few more examples:

use ≠ juice	*yoke ≠ joke*
yard ≠ jarred	*Yale ≠ jail*
yacht ≠ jot	*yell ≠ gel*
yaw ≠ jaw	*you ≠ jew*
yin ≠ gin	*yet ≠ jet*

  Furthermore, this consonant is typically followed by the long vowel /u:/ in different spellings: **"u"** (*student*), **"ew"** (*new*), **"iew"** (*interview*), **"eu"** (*Europe*), and **"eau"** (*beautiful*).

- As previously explained, **/ʤ/** is the voiced counterpart of /ʧ/, which appears in the words *James, joke, jeep*, and is the same sound as the Spanish /j/ in the words *yo* and *mayo* but with more emphasis. The most common spellings are **"g"**, **"j"**, **"ge"**, **"dg"**: *gym, june, age, badge*.

EXERCICES: 

1-. Listen to the minimal pairs containing /j/ and /ʤ/ and select in which order they are pronounced; write 1 for the first word you hear and 2 for the second:

your	2	yolk	yam
jaw	1	joke	jam
yak		year	
Jack		jeer	
Yale		yin	
jail		gin	
you		yet	
Jew		jet	

2-. Write the spelling of the words corresponding to the following transcriptions and put them in the correct column:

/ˈlɔːjə/; /juːs/; /ˈmeɪʤə/; /mjuːs/; /edjʊˈkeɪʃən/; /ˈmæʤɪk/; /keɪʤ/; /ˈævənjuː/; /ˈɑːgjuː/; /ˈnefjuː/; /ʤʌnʤ/; /frɪʤ/; /ˈbjuːtɪ/

/j/	/ʤ/
lawyer /ˈlɔːjə/	

3-. Tick the word that you hear in the sentences:

When are you going to ______?	Yale	☐	jail	☐
She doesn't like______.	yolks	☐	jokes	☐
______, come with me.	yes	☐	Jess	☐
I don't want to remember those ______ .	years	☐	jeers	☐
What ______ is that?	use	☐	juice	☐
That ______ is really tough.	yob	☐	job	☐

4-. Identify the words in the tongue-twister containin the given sound. Then practice and compare with the recording.

> *Jane can juggle jars.*
> *Jim can do gymnastics.*
> *John can jump joyfully, and James can jog largely on jagged hills.*
> *What do you judge Jess and Jenny can generally do? They generously join Jazz.*

Sound pair 8. RAN OR RANG? Sounds /n/ and /ŋ/

/ðə ˈsɪŋər ɪz ˈsɪŋɪŋ maɪ ˈfeɪvərɪt sɒŋ/

Visual cue: *the singer is singing my favourite song*

- In both Spanish and English there are the consonants /**m**/ and /**n**/, which are nasal sounds (when you pronounce them, the air goes out through your nose: see Annex 3).

- Whereas Spanish has got the nasal sound *ñ*, in English there is the /ŋ/ as in *ring*. It is a velar consonant, which means that the back of the tongue is raised towards the soft palate or velum: see Annex 3). /ŋ/ only occurs in Spanish as the result of an assimilation process in natural speech, that is, when *n* is followed by "k" or "g", as in *tango* /taŋgo/. The pronunciation of English /ŋ/is easy to imitate then; start saying the Spanish word *tango* and stop after the first syllable (/taŋ/).

- In English, /ŋ/ never appears in word initial position and is always followed by "g" or "k" in the spelling. The /k/ sound after /ŋ/ (in spelling **"nk"**) is always pronounced, as in *thanks* (/θæŋks/). However, the pronunciation of /g/ after /ŋ/ (in spelling **"ng"**) varies according to the following rules:

  - In word final position, the /g/ is never produced: *long* (/lɒŋ/), *running* (/ˈrʌnɪŋ/).

  - In word medial position, it is not produced if the word derives from a verb: *singing* (/ˈsɪŋɪŋ/), *singer* (/ˈsɪŋə/), *bringing* (/ˈbrɪŋɪŋ/).

  - In word medial position, it is pronounced if the word is not derived from a verb: *longer* (/ˈlɒŋgə/), *finger* (/ˈfɪŋgə/), *stronger* /strɒŋgə/.

  *The most common mistake for some Spanish speakers is to pronounce the /ŋ/ sound as simply /n/ in English words. This can lead to mistakes or cause intelligibility problems since pairs such as *ran* (/ræn/) and *rang* (/ræŋ/) may be confused. Other examples: *sun/sung, sin/sing, hand/hanged.*

  **In other cases, to make sure that the /ŋ/ is properly produced, speakers tend to produce the consonants /k/ or /g/ after /ŋ/. Be careful since, as shown above, this is right only in certain words (all those with spelling "nk". Those with "ng" the "g" is rarely pronounced, depending on the rules explained).

EXERCICES: 

1-. You will hear two words from the box. If you hear the same word twice, write S (same). If you hear two different words, write D (different): e.g. 1 *thin/thing*: D.

thing/think; win/wing; sinner/singer; singing/sinking; Ron/wrong; ban/bank

2.   3.

4.   5.

6.   7.

2-. Listen and choose the word or phrase you hear:

sinners/singers/sinkers
win/wing/wink
ban/bank/bang
sun/sung/sunk
thin/thing/think
ran/rang/rank

He ran/rang home yesterday.
That can't be Ron/wrong.
Don't ban/bang it!
She's singing/sinking in the bath.

3-. Listen to the refrain from Britney Spears' song "Stronger" and complete the lyrics:

_________ *than yesterday*
Now it's _________ *but my way*
My loneliness ain't _________ *me no more*
I, I'm _________

Sound pair 9. GOOD OR WOULD? Sounds /g/ and /w/

Would (modal verb)
Avoid saying *good* (/gʊd/) g ❌

a wonderful white whale
Visual cue: *a <u>w</u>onderful <u>wh</u>ite <u>wh</u>ale*

- The English consonant **/w/**, which appears at the beginning of words such as *week* or *whisky*, has a similar quality to the short vowel /ʊ/ and is also called a **semivowel**. It is normally spelt **"w"** or **"wh"** and sometimes **"u"** (following /k/ or /g/, that is, the combinations "qu" and "gu" which are pronounced /kw/ and /gw/): *queen, quiet, language, penguin*. There are English words where the spelling "w" is **silent,** as in the combinations "wr" and "wh" *(write, who)*, and the words *answer* or *two*. Finally, the sound /w/ is not always obvious from a word's spelling: e.g. *one*.

*A common mistake for some Spanish speakers is to pronounce /w/ as the velar /g/, that is, the consonant in which the back of the tongue is raised towards the soft palate or velum (see Annex 3). As a result, you might be saying *guest* (/gest/)

rather than *west* (/west/). More problematic is when Spanish people say *good* (/gʊd/) rather than *would* (/wʊd/) any time they use the modal verb.

****/w/ is both a **labio-dental** and **velar** sound, which means that your teeth must touch your lips before your tongue moves towards the velum (see Annex 3). However, be careful not to confuse /w/ with the other labio-dental consonant /v/, which can also cause mistakes: e.g. the distinction between *The dog's vet* and *The dog's wet*.

Therefore, for the production of English /w/, make a similar sound to /ʊ/ and make sure that your teeth and lips come together.

EXERCICES: 

1-. Write the spelling of the words corresponding to the following transcriptions:

/kwɪk/; /kwiːn/; /kəˈləʊkwiəl/; /ˈædɪkwət/; /ˈkwɒtɪ/; /ˈlæŋgwɪdʒ/; /ˈpeŋgwɪn/; /ˈlɪŋgwɪst/

2-. In each group of words, three of them begin with the same consonant and the other has a different sound. Find the odd one out and explain which is the difference.

water	whale	whole	window
when	who	where	which
write	one	world	waste

3-. Practice the /w/ sound through the following well-known tongue-twister. At first, read it slowly, as many times as necessary. When you pronounce the sentences correctly and fluently, you can increase the speed level. Then compare with the recording in the key.

How much wood would a woodchuck chuck if a woodchuck could chuck wood? He would chuck as much wood as a woodchuck could chuck.

4-. Choose the word that you hear:

vine/wine; veal/wheel; veil/whale;

invite/in white; vet/wet; verse/worse

5-. Tick the word that you hear in the following pairs containing either /g/ or /w/:

gate	☐	wait	☐
got	☐	what	☐
gun	☐	one	☐
guy	☐	why	☐
get	☐	wet	☐
gone	☐	won	☐

Sound pair 10. EAR OR HEAR? Sound /h/

a huge, hollow horse

Visual cue: *a huge, hollow horse*

"Henry's horse has hurt his hoof in a hole while hunting. Henry helps him to hobble home." /ˈhenrɪz hɔː s əz hɜː t ɪz ˈhuː f ɪn ə ˈhəʊl waɪl ˈhʌntɪŋ | ˈhenri ˈhelps ɪm tə ˈhɒbl həʊm/ (Trim 2001, p. 77)

Read the text above with the aid of the transcription and record it. Now compare your recording with this one (Do you think that you pronounced the /h/ sound correctly?):

- The most common pronunciation of **/h/** corresponds to the letter or grapheme **"h"**: *hat, horse, behind, perhaps*. Other possible spelling is **"wh"**: *whole, who, whose*. There are some English words where the spelling "h" is **silent**: *hour, honest, heir*.

*One of the typical mistakes is the mispronunciation of the English consonant **/h/** (in the word *hotel*) when confused with the Spanish /x/ (in the word *jaula*). The production of the English /h/ is not as strong as the Spanish /x/; in fact, it makes very little sound as it is similar to the expulsion of air through the mouth through your breath. Look at the BBC video:

/h/ is commonly **dropped in the pronunciation of pronouns and auxiliary verbs as long as they are not at the beginning of a sentence. Listen to some examples:

Is he Thomas?   *Do you know him?*
Have you seen her?   *He was staying with his friends.*
Has he already arrived? *I am waiting for her.*

Listen to the following pairs of words. Can you hear the difference?

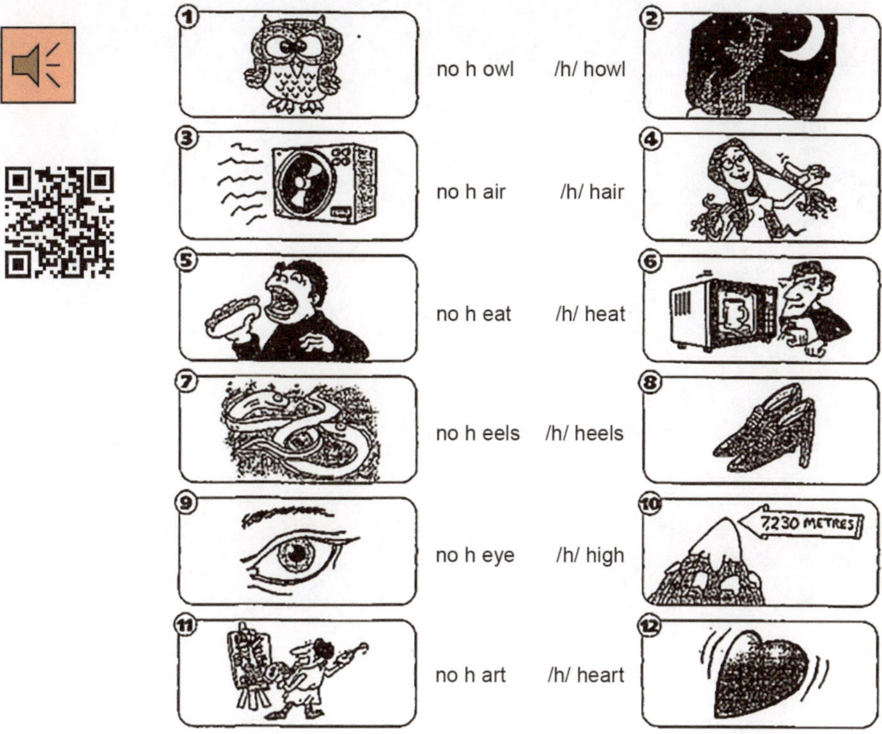

Picture: *Timesaver Pronunciation Activities* (2005), by Bill Bowler, p. 60

EXERCICES:

1-. In each group of words, three of them begin with the same consonant and the other has a different sound. Find the odd one out and explain which is the difference:

hour	*half*	*home*	*high*
how	*honest*	*healthy*	*happy*

2-. Identify the sequences where /h/ is dropped and transcribe them. Listen and check:

/h/ in the pronoun is dropped: /ˈtel ə/

tell her   *ask her sister*   *her sister*
tell him   *ask his sister*   *his sister*

3-. Listen and choose the word you hear:

old/hold and/hand ill/hill eating/ heating   eight/hate art/heart

4-. Tick the word that you hear:

eat	☐	heat	☐
Ellen	☐	Helen	☐
old	☐	hold	☐
ill	☐	hill	☐
air	☐	hair	☐
ate	☐	hate	☐
art	☐	heart	☐
all	☐	hall	☐
eye	☐	high	☐

UK OR US ENGLISH? Sound /r/

Visual cue: *a far away star*

Picture: *English Pronunciation Illustrated* (2001), by John Trim, p. 73

In Spanish there are two types of *r* sounds: a 'stronger' one (called alveolar roll), which appears in the words *ratón* and *carro* (spelling: initial "r" or "rr"), and the one in *pera* or *María* (corresponding to intervocalic "r" in spelling and called alveolar flap).

In English, the pronunciation of *r* is quite different as it is a **post-alveolar** consonant, which means that the tip of the tongue is held just behind (not touching, as in Spanish) the alveolar ridge (see Annex 3). Besides, the back edges of the tongue touche the upper molars (top back teeth). The soft palate is raised.

/**r**/ is usually spelt **"r"** and **"rr"**: *Rome, read, train, sorry, mirror, hurry*. There are some other words with a very different spelling: **"wr"** (*write*) or **"rh"** (*rhyme*).

*In <u>RP English</u>, the standard English spoken in the United Kingdom, the /r/ is only pronounced when it is followed by a vowel (as in *red*: /red/) but not when it is followed by a consonant (as in *farm*: /fɑ:m/) or a pause (as in *far*: /fɑ:/). RP English is non-rhotic as opposed to rhotic accents such as Irish, Scottish or <u>American English</u>, where the /r/ is pronounced in all cases.

However, in RP English /r/ is also frequently pronounced due to connected speech, that is, when words form part of a phrase or sentence and the /r/ sound is followed by a word beginning with a vowel (eg *far away*, *for example*, *the car is blue* or the *door is open*). This phenomenon is called "linking r**". Listen to some examples:

RP English	American English
for: no /r/	*for:* /r/ is pronounced
forty: no /r/	*forty:* /r/ is pronounced
for them: no /r/	*for them:* /r/ is pronounced
for Allan: /r/ is pronounced	*for Allan:* /r/ is pronounced
for hours: /r/ is pronounced	*for hours:* /r/ is pronounced

EXERCICES: 

1-. Listen to the following words and decide whether they are produced in RP English or American English; you should pay attention to the presence of the /r/ before a consonant or a pause (AE) or not (RP).

word: AE   *girl:*
start   *teacher:*
door: *calendar:*
bird: *curl:*
storm: *hammer:*

2-. Go to Voicetube and look for authentic videoclips with speakers from different countries or with different accents. Find examples of rhotic and non-rothic language and the use of 'linking r'.

3-. The following sentences contain several words which can be pronounced with a *linking r* (when /r/ is followed by a vowel). Look at the words with final "r" in the spelling and put a tick if it is pronounced and a cross otherwise, e.g.:
I don't remember ✓it well but you could be right after ✓all.

1. *The doctor will arrive later on.*
2. *My father and my mother are waiting for us.*
3. *Are you far away from here?*
4. *Is there any sugar in the cupboard?*
5. *The car is out of order.*
6. *You are as smart as your mother.*
7. *The teacher and the students are in the History museum today.*
8. *There are more pencils over there.*
9. *The letter arrived before I moved.*
10. *Our aunt always gives us a bar of chocolate.*

3. MORPHEMIC RULES

[HOW TO AVOID] COMMON MISTAKES

- ✗ Common mistake: *stopped* → /stɒped/; *dogs* → /dɒgs/

- ✓ Correct pronunciation: *stopped* → /stɒpt/; *dogs* → /dɒgz/

- ☞ Explanation: typical mistakes for Spanish speakers include the mispronunciation of past or plural morphemes, that is, the "-ed" and "-s" endings we add to words to form the regular past or the plural in English.

   As students are misled by the graphemes or spelling of the words and may not know the pronunciation rules, "-ed", for example, is usually pronounced as /ed/ while the correct pronunciation should be /t/, /d/ or / /ɪd/ depending on the verb.

   In the case of the "-s" morpheme, the main mistake lies in pronouncing in all cases the voiceless consonant /s/ as in Spanish, failing to recognize where a different phoneme, voiced /z/, should be used in English.

3 ways of pronouncing "ed" (/t/, /d/, /ɪd/). Picture from Youtube channel (English with Lucy)

In this unit, you will learn about the pronunciation of morphemic aspects of the English language, which are crucial to know as they appear in the most basic grammar structures:

1. The ending "-ed", which is necessary for the formation of the regular past and past participle (*started*) and which also appears in many adjectives (*depressed, bored*).
2. The ending "-s", which is necessary for the formation of the plurals and the present tense (*cats*; *she likes*), among others.

To correctly apply the morphemic rules, first you need to know or remember the following classification of sounds in voiceless and voiced:

> **Voiceless**: /p, t, k, ʧ , f, θ, s, ʃ, h/
> **Voiced**: /b, d, g, ʤ, v, ð, z, ʒ, m, n, ŋ, l, r, j, w/ + VOWELS + DIPTHONGS

I.   "-ed" MORPHEME

We add the morpheme "-ed" to form the past and past participle of all regular verbs but this ending is pronounced in 3 different ways according to the following rules:

- If the previous sound is voiceless,[1] the final "-ed" is pronounced /t/:

  For example, in *walk* the last sound is /k/ so for the pronunciation of the regular past (*walked*), we should add /t/ at the end: /wɔːkt/

  * As you can see, there is no vowel here, that is, avoid saying /wɔːkɪt/.

  ** Pay attention to the last sound of the verb rather than the spelling: e.g. in *laugh* the last sound is "f", that is why the regular past is pronounced /lɑːft/.

  Other examples: *shopped, stopped, picked, coughed, fished.*

- If the previous sound is voiced, the final "-ed" is pronounced /d/:

  For example, in *rain* the last sound is /n/ so for the pronunciation of the regular past (*rained*), we should add /d/ at the end: /reɪnd/.

  *Again, there is no vowel here (avoid saying /reɪnɪd/).

  Other examples: *lived, chilled, enjoyed, played.*

- If the previous sound is /t/ or /d/, the final "-ed" is pronounced:

  For example, the last sounds in *want* and *end* are /t/ and /d/ respectively, so for the pronunciation of the regular past (*wanted* and *ended*), we should add /ɪd/: /wɒntɪd/, /endɪd/.

  *This is the only case in which there is a vowel: *visited*→ /vɪzɪtɪd/.

  Other examples: *needed, hated, dated, seated.*

  **Note that when we pronounce "ed" as /ɪd/, there is also an extra syllable. Listen and compare the following examples (from Hancock 2012, p. 56) using a verb in the present and past respectively:

  I wait(ed) and count(ed) to ten.

  The games start(ed) early and end(ed) late.

  They heat(ed) the coffee and add(ed) milk.

  We want(ed) to pay but we need(ed) more money.

---

[1] The reference is the original word (the word before you add the morpheme); in this case, the infinitive of the verb.

EXERCICES: 

1-. Listen to what Callum did last Sunday. In particular listen to how he pronounces the "-ed" endings of the regular past simple verbs. Which group does each verb fall into: /t/, /d/ or /ɪd/? Fill in the chart as in the example (Source: BBC Learning English):

Sunday (1) turned into a very long day. My mum was coming back from holiday so I went to the airport to pick her up. Unfortunately her flight was (2) delayed for a couple hours so I had to hang around at the airport. I went to the bookshop and (3) browsed around for a while, (4) flicked through some magazines and bought a paper to read while I (5) waited. home because she was so tired. So we (8) jumped in the car and I (9) dropped her off at her place. Then (10) headed to my flat in south London but when I (11) tried to find my house keys, they weren't in my pocket. I (12) realised with horror that I must have left them in the airport bookshop when I was paying for my paper. So I had to go all the way back to the airport but luckily someone had handed in my keys and I was able to collect them and come home again. It was a very, very long day.

(1) *turned*: /d/	(4) *flicked*: ____	(7) *wanted*: ____	(10) *headed*: ____
(2) *delayed*: ____	(5) *waited*: ____	(8) *jumped*: ____	(11) *tried*: ____
(3) *browsed*: ____	(6) *arrived*: ____	(9) *dropped*: ____	(12) *realised*: ____

2-. Choose the word that is pronounced differently from the others:

talked	fished	arrived	stepped
wished	wrapped	laughed	turned
consider	rescued	pulled	rushed
delivered	organized	replaced	obeyed
painted	provided	protected	equipped
tested	marked	presented	founded
used	finished	married	rained
allowed	dressed	flashed	mixed
switched	stayed	beieved	cleared

3-. Listen and circle the verb tense you hear: present or past.

I always walk/walked on my own here.
I always want/wanted to talk to you.
Me and my friends play/played a lot.
On Saturday, we dance/danced all night!
I never call/called you at night.
They never help/helped me.
I enjoy/enjoyed eating out.
They follow/followed my advice.

4-. Tell your favourite story or tale when you were a child by only using verbs in their regular past form. Record it and listen to it after a few days to check whether your pronunciation of the "-ed" ending is correct.

5-. Listen and complete the sentences with the verb tense you hear: present or past.

We usually finished before the others.
You _______ the wrong question.
I _______ a new item to the list.
I _______ the opera but the breaks _______ too long.

I _______ the news with you.
We _______ for miles and miles.
They usually _______ up early.
I _______ the hospital on my way to work.

6-. Read aloud and record the sentences on the second column below. Make sure you pronounce the "-ed" ending correctly. It is very important to convey the correct meaning because it shows that the action is in the past rather than in the present. Then check with the audio provided in the Key section and listen to the differences in the pronunciation of the sentences depending on the tense (did you pronounce your own sentences in the present or the past?).

* If you find it difficult to say the "-ed" ending, you can add the corresponding sound to the next word in a sentence, e.g. *I looked everywhere* as '*I look **t**everywhere*' or *I explained it* as '*I explain **dit**'.

VERB TENSE:	PRESENT	PAST
	You never lie to me.	*You never lied to me.*
	I usually listen to music.	*I usually listened to music.*
	We always phone our parents.	*We always phoned our parents.*

II. "-s" MORPHEME

the witch's roses
/ðə ˈwɪtʃɪz ˈrəʊzɪz/

Visual cue: *the witch's roses*

We add morphemic "-s" in the following circumstances:

- to form the plural of nouns: *dog-dogs, cat-cats.*

- in the third person singular of verbs in present tense: *goes, walks.*

- in saxon genitive (possessives): *Tim's, Kate's.*

- in contractions (e.g. "is" and "has"): *it's blue, he's got a car.*

Just the same as with the "-ed" morpheme, the pronunciation of morphemic "-s" varies and follows similar rules. There are also 3 possible pronunciations:

- If the previous sound is voiceless,[2] the final "-s" is pronounced /s/:

For example, the last sounds in *cat* and *want* are /t/, so for the pronunciation of the plural in *cats* and the third person of the present tense verb *wants*, we should add /s/.

Other examples: *walks, shops, stops, clocks.*

- If the previous sound is voiced, the final "-s" is pronounced /z/:

For example, the last sounds in *dog* and *rain* are /g/ and /n/ respectively, so for the pronunciation of *dogs* and *rains*, we should add /z/.

Other examples: *enjoys, moons, dolls, cars.*

- If the previous sound is sibilant (/s, z, ʃ, ʒ, ʧ, dʒ/), the final "-s" is pronounced /ɪz/:

For example, the last sounds in *kiss* is /s/, so for the pronunciation of the plural or verb (*two kisses* or *She kisses*), we should add /ɪz/.

Other examples: *roses, kisses, roses, fishes, churches, judges, witches, watches.*

*is and *has* are not contracted after a sibilant consonant, e.g. *The food's good vs The service is good; the game's started vs The match has started.*

**Note that when we pronounce "-s" as /ɪz/, there is an extra syllable. For example, the name *Chris* has one syllable, but the possessive *Chris's* has two syllables.

Listen and notice how the "-s" ending changes the meaning in the following examples (Hancock 2012, p. 54).

WORD CATEGORY:	NOUN	VERB
	Jane's nose	*Jane knows*
	Nick's weights	*Nick waits*
GRAMMATICAL NUMBER:	SINGULAR	PLURAL
	My friend spends a lot	*My friends spend a lot*
	Our guest came late	*Our guests came late*

---

[2] The reference is the original word (the word before you add the morpheme); in this case, it can be the noun (*cat*), the verb (*walk*), the proper noun for the possessive (*Tom*) and the subject (*it; he*).

EXERCICES: 

1-. Choose the word that is pronounced differently from the others:

sees	*sings*	*meets*	*needs*
seeks	*plays*	*gets*	*looks*
tries	*receives*	*teache*	*studies*
says	*pays*	*stays*	*pets*
eyes	*apples*	*tables*	*faces*
posts	*types*	*wives*	*keeps*
beds	*pens*	*notebooks*	*rulers*
buses	*crashes*	*bridges*	*plates*
parks	*animals*	*planets*	*tops*
helps	*provides*	*documents*	*texts*

2-. Listen and choose the word you hear. Then practice saying the words making the difference between /s/ and /z/ clear.

Singular noun + contraction	*scarf's*	*knife's*	*thief's*	*half's*	*wife's*	*life's*	*calf's*
Irregular plural noun	*scarves*	*knives*	*thieves*	*halves*	*wives*	*lives*	*calves*

3-. Listen to these extracts from Avicii's song "The nights" and write which pronunciations of the "-s" morpheme (/s/, /z/ or /ɪz/) you hear:

"The nights"

Once upon a younger year
When all our shadows disappered

The animals inside came out to play
Went face to face with all our fears.
Learned out lessons through the tears
Made memories we knew would
never fade.

One day, my father, he told me,
'Son, don't let it slip away

He took me in his arms,
I heard him say
'When you get older your wild
heart will live for younger days'

'When thunderclouds start
pouring down

Light a fire they can't put out
Carve your name into those
shining stars'
He said 'Go venture far
beyond the shores

Don't forsake this life of
yours

I'll guide you home, no matter
where you are'

He said 'One day, you'll leave this
world behind

So live a life you will remember'
My father told me when I was just a
child

These are the nights that never die
My father told me

These are the nights that never die
My father told me
My father told me

4-. Classify the words given according to the pronunciation rules of the "-s" morpheme previously explained (there is only one possible square for each word except for one extra):

weeks; drinks; watches; Rose's; John's; eggs; it's; wages; Mark's; wins; she's

	/s/	/z/	/ɪz/
plurals			
present simple			
possessive			
is/has contractions			

5-. Find a route from the start to the end. Moves can be horizontal, vertical or diagonal but you may pass a square only if the "-s" morpheme in it is pronounced in the same way as the previous word.

START

clocks	drinks	moves	dolls	washes
gloves	shops	starts	sinks	rabbits
plays	kisses	clowns	cars	months
feels	roses	comes	girls	jokes
draws	boxes	dares	beers	books

END

6-. Transcribe the following plurals and verbs by paying attention to the three different pronunciations of the "-s" morpheme: /s/, /z/ or /ız/.

judges:	*watches:*
lives:	*attends:*
plates:	*tapes:*
classes:	*books:*
breathes:	*wives:*
shines:	*churches:*
rays:	*puts:*
rocks:	*watches:*
eggs:	*manages:*
orders:	*hours:*
buses:	*pitches:*
goes:	*bushes:*
cows:	*laughs:*
steaks:	*stores:*
hates:	*rings:*

7-. Transcribe the following sentence and explain the rules of the "-s" morpheme in relation to the verb *speaks* and the plural *languages*:

Jim speaks three languages

4. STRESS

[HOW TO AVOID] COMMON MISTAKES

> ✗Common mistake: *sofa, periphery, Canterbury* → /souˈfa/, /periˈferɪ/, /kanˈterburɪ/

> ✓ Correct pronunciation: /ˈsəʊfə/, /pəˈrɪfərɪ/, /ˈkæntəbrɪ/

> ☞ Explanation: the stress distribution in English and Spanish may vary, even if the words look similar in both languages. A common mistake for Spanish speakers is to apply the stress distribution of Spanish words to the English ones, which may result in being perceived with a foreign accent. Therefore, it is very important for students to know how words are pronounced not only in terms of vowels and consonants but paying attention to stress.

In this unit you will learn about the different stress patterns in English and Spanish, which is particularly important in natural speech. The main difference is that English is a stressed-timed language whereas Spanish is a syllable-timed language.

Stress is the degree of emphasis given to a sound or syllable in speech. A stressed syllable is indicated with the symbol /ˈ/; e.g., in *better*, the stressed syllable is the first one and the unstressed syllable has got the weak vowel schwa: /ˈbetə/.

In English, stress influences several aspects of pronunciation such as the length (stressed syllables are longer) and, most importantly, the quality of vowels (unstressed syllables have weak vowels like the 'schwa').

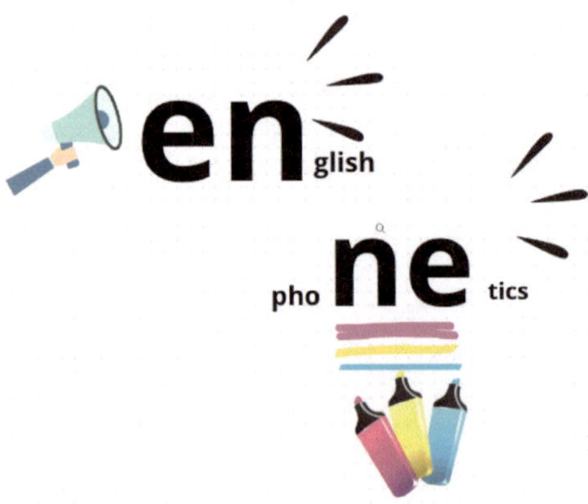

I.   WORD STRESS

When words are pronounced in isolation (not in a phrase or sentence), all words have at least one stressed syllable.

In polysyllabic words (with more than one syllable), one of the syllables bears the accent (the stressed syllable or strongly stressed syllable) and the others are unstressed (the weakly stressed syllables). For example, *answer* bears the stress on the first syllable while *again* carries it on the second. Three-syllable words may present the following **stress patterns** (the mark ' is used to indicate stressed syllables and the big circles represent also the stressed syllable while the small circles indicate the unstressed/weakly stressed syllables):

1. O o o (*saturday, hospital*) /ˈsætədeɪ/
2. o O o (*computer, unhappy*) /kəmˈpjuːtə/
3. o o O (*understand, afternoon*) /ɑːftəˈnuːn/

*As you can see, very frequently the unstressed syllable contains the **weak vowel shwa**. This can help you a great deal to predict pronunciation and avoid very common mistakes. For example, many Spanish speakers may mispronounce the word *London* by giving the same emphasis to both of the syllables and vowels. Only the first syllable is stressed and the two vowels, although spelt the same, are pronounced totally differently: the first "o" has a clear, strong sound (/ɒ/) while the second has a weak sound (/ə/). Note how the shwa is actually scarcely audible or difficult to hear, especially in sentences or connected speech (Marks 2007, p. 16) , as is explained in the next section (Sentence stress):

London   *banana*
I have to go to London tomorrow   *Would you like a banana?*

This explains why you may find it difficult to recognize certain words when listening to native speakers. Therefore this unit is extremely important if you want to improve your listening skills in English, but also your pronunciation by clearly differentiating between stressed (strong) syllables and unstressed (weak) syllables.

** Careful with spelling! The number of syllables in a word is based on the number of vowel sounds (not letters). This means that monosyllabic words can be really long when spelt: e.g. *fields* (6 letters but only one syllable). Compare also:

- *worked*: 2 vowel letters but only 1 vowel sound, so 1 syllable → /ˈwɜːkt/
- *different*: 3 vowel letters but only 2 vowel sounds, so 2 syllables → /ˈdɪfrənt/

Sometimes the consonants /n/ and /l/ can be syllabic too, that is, fill the space of a vowel in a syllable. When /ə/ is followed by /n/ or /l/, the schwa may disappear, although the number of syllables stays the same: *sudden* (/ˈsʌ/+/dən/=/ˈsʌ/+/dn/, 2 syllables); *people*

(/ˈpiː/+/pəl/ = /ˈpiː/+/pl̩/, 2 syllables); *syllable* (/ˈsɪ/ +/lə/ +/bəl/=/ˈsɪ/ +/lə/ +/bl̩/, 3 syllables).

Stress patterns can help you distinguish between similar words, e.g. numbers ending in *-teen* and *-ty*. Listen:

o O	O o
thirteen	*thirty*
fourteen	*fourty*
sixteen	*sixty*
eighteen	*eighty*
nineteen	*ninety*

II.   SENTENCE STRESS

Visual cue: *Would you like a piece of cake?* (weak forms)

When words are pronounced together inside phrases or sentences in connected speech, some words retain their stress and others lose it. For example, in *The 'fight between the 'cat and the 'dog*, there are only three stressed syllables/words (*fight, cat* and *dog*). The grammar word *between* loses its stress (in isolation, the stress would be on the second syllable: /bɪˈtwiːn/).

Many words in English are unstressed when used in sentences. For example, pronounced in isolation, the prepositions *to* and *for* sound like the numbers *two* and *four* (/tuː/ and /fɔː/. However, normally these words are used in sentences and are unstressed (pronounced with a swcha: /tə/ and /fə/).

As just said, when words are isolated, all words are stressed. However, in connected speech there are words which are rarely stressed. The words which are usually **unstressed** are **grammar words**, those that have little lexical meaning and are pronounced in their **weak forms**[1]: prepositions, pronouns, auxiliary and modal verbs, conjunctions and articles. The pronunciation of all the weakly stressed words is fast and scarcely audible;

---

[1] See also next unit for a more detailed explanation.

and even when we add more unstressed words to a sentence, we still say it in about the same length of time by speaking more quickly and quietly.

By contrast, the most important words in a sentence are **strongly stressed**. They are pronounced louder and slower. These words, which often keep the stress in connected speech because they carry considerable semantic weight, are **lexical or content words**: nouns, main verbs, adjectives and adverbs.

In natural speech, when you hear sentences in English, you hear the combination of stressed and unstressed words and syllables as a stress pattern. This is what creates **rhythm** in English, which is a stressed-timed language unlike Spanish (syllable-timed).

Listen to these sentences while looking at the stress patterns and notice how the weak stresses are quicke r and quieter or less perceptible. *o* represents unstressed syllables; these may be whole words or syl lables of a longer word: e.g., the phrase *middle of the night* hast got this stress pa ttern: OoooO. The three *ooo* are the second syllable of *middle* and the unstressed grammar words   *of* and *the*).

1: oOOo *It's not spicy.*
2: oooOOo *What are you doing tonight?*
3: OooOo *Write me a letter.*
4: OoooO *Put it in a box.*
5: OoOOo *Drive the car slowly.*
6: ooOoO *I can see your home.*

III.   STRESS IN SPEECH UNITS

When we speak, we do not only use sentences but engage in longer conversations. Long messages are often divided into shorter speech units or **groups of words** to facilitate understanding. Speech units are normally marked by punctuation in written English such as the pauses done through commas or full stops, although in spoken English there may be more cases in which speakers decide to 'break' the message and pause (e.g., for emphasis).

In every speech unit, only one syllable or word has the **main stress**: it tends to be the **last content word** or one of the syllables in it if it is a polysyllabic word. For example, the long sentence *I was waiting for ages and the music was so loud, so I decided to leave without them* can be divided into three speech units as follows:

- *I was waiting for ages:* the main stress is on the stressed syllable of the last content word.

- *and the music was so loud:* the main stress is on the last content word.

- *so I decided to leave without them:* the main stress is not on the last word if it is a grammar word; therefore, the main stress is on the last content word.

EXERCICES: 

1-. Arrange the words in the box according to their stress pattern (if necessary, use the transcription bank given to help you):

direction; furniture; begin; please; clear; anyone; remember; yesterday; November; tomorrow; accept; incredible; bank; beautiful; above; intentional; collect

O	oO	oOo	oOoo	Ooo
cut	*explain*	*amazing*	*impossible*	*suitable*

/ˈbjuːtɪfʊl/;/kəˈlekt/; /pliːz/; /bɪˈɡɪn/; /inˈkredəbl/; /əˈbʌv/; /ˈjestədi/; /əkˈsept/; /nəˈvembə/; /ɪnˈtenʃənl/; /ˈfɜːnɪtʃə/; /ˈeniwʌn/; /klɪə/; /dɪˈrekʃən/; /bæŋk/; /riˈmembə/; /təˈmɒrəu/

2-. Some words in each of these lists have the same stress pattern. Find the odd one out (the big and small circles represent the stressed and unstressed syllables respectively):

oO	*repeat*	*above*	*hotel*	*acquire*	*Texas*
Oo	*service*	*building*	*Japan*	*answer*	*about*
oOo	*politics*	*essential*	*tomato*	*december*	*policeman*
Ooo	*wonderful*	*computer*	*yesterday*	*regular*	*possible*
ooOo	*information*	*contribution*	*understanding*	*impossible*	*inexpensive*

3-. Find the fish which is caught in this pronunciation game designed by Mark Hancock (1995, p. 85) and also used as a communicative activity (Harmer 2001, p. 257) by matching the sentences/phrases according to their stress pattern:

4-. Classify these sentences according to their stress pattern:

The train was late.   *Come and try.*   *Close the window.*   *What do you think?*
The water's hot.   *Give me a chance!*   *What did he say?*   *Phone and tell me.*
Nice to meet you.   *Where's the car?*   *It's cold and wet.*   *What's the time?*

OooO	oOoO	OoO	OoOo
	The train was late.		

5-. Listen to this story and identify the main stresses in the speech units marked by the speaker. After you check with the Key, practice <u>reading aloud</u> the story; you can do so together <u>with the recording</u> so that you imitate better the rhythm and pace you should follow. It is useful to rewrite the story with each speech unit on a separate line so that you can easily see where to pause, put the stress and show emphasis:

Get the strangers out of our house! That's, believe it or not, how my grandmother would greet my friends. As you can imagine, I wasn't really fond of her. This is a photo of my grandmother, on her fourth birthday in 1909 in New York City. When I was 16, I found out that the day after this picture was taken, she was kidnapped, abducted by one of the gangs of extortionists known as the Black Hand that pried on Little Italies. They had her 3 months and it was only because of the strength and cunning of my great-grandmother that she was returned to life. It took me years to get the full story, but when I did I was finally able to love my grandmother and to understand the transformative power of knowing you family history.

<u>Get the strangers</u>
out of our <u>house!</u>
<u>That</u>
<u>believe</u> it or not
is how my <u>grandmother</u>
would <u>greet</u> my <u>friends</u>
...

Source: extract from "A genealogical journey", by Laurie Fabiano
(https://www.youtube.com/watch?v=KpiSxFSYxUY&ab_channel=TEDArchive)

5. CONNECTED SPEECH

[HOW TO AVOID] COMMON MISTAKES

◊ **MIND THE DIFFERENT RHYTHM**

Spanish syllable-timed rhythm vs English stress-timed rhythm

✘ Common mistake:
  Jonathan will arrive tomorrow afternoon: /ˈjonatan ˈwil aˈraif tuˈmorou afterˈnun/

✓ Correct pronunciation:
  /ˈdʒɒnəθən wɪl əˈraɪv təˈmɒrəʊ ɑːftəˈnuːn/

✘ Common mistake:
  Little old lady: /ˈlitel ˈold ˈleɪdɪ/

✓ Correct pronunciation:
  /ˈlɪtəl əʊld ˈleɪdɪ/

☞ Explanation: the previous examples (Estebas-Vilaplana 2009) show a crucial contrast many speakers are not aware of regarding suprasegmental features of pronunciation, such as rhythm and stress. Comprehension problems are often more attributed to these components than to inaccuracies in the pronunciation of individual sounds (Nunan 2015, p. 96). We tend to wrongly assume that rhythm in English is syllabic as in Spanish, where all syllables take approximately the same amount of time or all syllables (stressed and unstressed) have a similar duration. English is a stress-timed language, that is, it is based on stress, whereas Spanish is a syllable-timed language, which means that the syllables (no matter whether stressed or unstressed) are produced at equal time intervals. In English, only the stressed syllables tend to be produced at equal time intervals.

In spoken English sentences, the most important words for the speaker are strongly stressed. The important words are those that have meaning in a sentence (nouns, verbs, adjectives and adverbs) and are called content words, by contrast to the grammar words (articles, conjunctions, pronouns, prepositions, auxiliary and modal verbs) which only have a grammatical function and are generally unstressed. Strongly stressed words are 'LOUDER' and 's l o w e r' or 'l o n g e r'. Weakly stressed words are quieter and quicker. This gives English its rhythm: there is the same amount of time between a stressed syllable and the next one, no matter the number of unstressed syllables in between, which means that the more unstressed syllables between stresses, the quicker they must be pronounced to maintain that similar time interval (making it a bit difficult to hear some words!). Another aspect derived from the stress-timed rhythm in English is that when there are three consecutive stressed content words, the one in middle tends to lose the stress. That is why in the phrase 'little old lady', old is unstressed even if it is a content word.

In this unit you will learn basic features of the English language that are extremely important if you want to improve both your listening and speaking skills. There are some rules that will help you understand better native speakers as well as boost your own fluency, especially by sounding more natural in the pronunciation of larger sequences of speech.

It is often said that English people speak very fast and that they 'swallow' the words. These are common complaints from students, even those at an advanced level, whose ignorance of the grammar and vocabulary used is not the reason for their lack of understanding.

If these students read a sentence in its written form, they have no comprehension problems but spoken English poses difficulties. This is not only because spelling differs from pronunciation, as it is explained in the previous units. The main reason is that **speech is a continuous stream of sounds** without clear borderlines between words.

When we write in English, each word is separate and there are spaces between the words. However, when we speak, although there are some pauses, we mostly bump the words together. As a consequence, a typical phenomenon is that consonant sounds link with vowel sounds and different words are pronounced as just one (e.g., *An* **egg** becomes '*anegg*').

Furthermore, because English is a stressed-timed language, speakers try to make the intervals between stressed syllables equal, which means they tend to actually 'swallow' **non-essential words**. This type of words are articles, conjunctions, pronouns, prepositions and auxiliary and modal verbs, that is, **grammar or function words**, which are words that do not have semantic content but have a more grammatical role in relating content or lexical words (those with semantic weight: nouns, verbs, adjectives and adverbs) or higher syntactic units in a sentence.

Grammar words are pronounced in their **weak forms** and some sounds are often lost or scarcely audible. Weak forms are characterized by the use of weak vowels (usually the schwa) and elision/disappearance of vowels and/or consonants.

This causes comprehension problems for students, particularly those whose language is syllable-timed such as Spanish. Remember that in English stress is very different: only the content or lexical words are stressed, that is, the most important words, those which really have meaning. Therefore, you must not only recognize these weak forms you hear but also use them when speaking English. Otherwise, you will sound unnatural (like a robot) with too many stressed forms, making it difficult for the listener to identify the points of focus (the important words).

Some examples of words which have weak forms are the prepositions *to* and *for*. If you say them in isolation, they sound like the numbers *two* and *four* (/tu:/ and /fɔ:/. However, normally these words are used in sentences and are pronounced differently (/tə/ and /fə/; with a swcha). In short, a change in vowel quality is common in the majority of the function or grammar words used in connected speech.

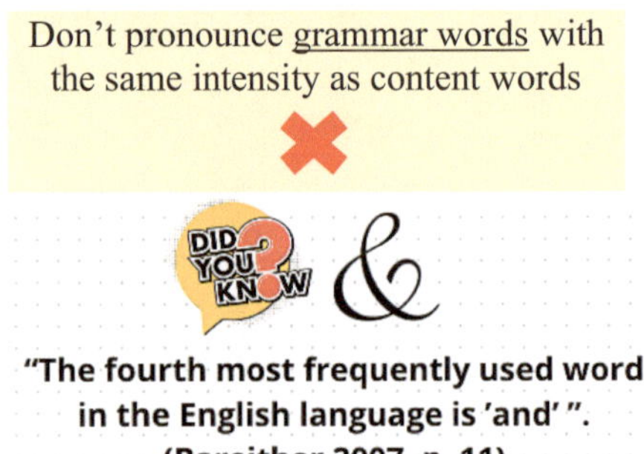

Notice the frequency of grammar words!

I. WEAK FORMS

The learning of weak forms is essential as it not only facilitates the correct production of sounds in English but also a proper understanding of native speakers. Generally, when we speak we do not produce words in isolation but as part of sentences. This is called connected speech, which changes the pronunciation of certain words. These are the grammar words, that is, prepositions, pronouns, auxiliary and modal verbs, conjunctions, articles, possessive and indefinite articles. These grammar words, in isolation, would be pronounced with a strong form but with a weak form in connected speech, as the following chart shows in the case of prepositions (for a complete list, see Annex 4):

Prepositions		
	Strong	Weak[1]
as	/ æz/	/əz/
at	/ /æt/	/ət/
for	/fɔ:/	/fə/
from	/frɒm/	/frəm/
of	/ɒv/	/əv/
to	/tu:/	/tə, tʊ/

In short, some words in connected speech are pronounced differently. For example, it is very usual to drop the /h/ of pronouns in phrases such as *hasn't he* or *tell him* (*he* →/ɪ/; *him* →/ɪm/). However, the situation is different if the pronoun appears at the beginning of a sentence (*He is Paul: he* → /hɪ/). This is because immediately following a pause it is not usual to omit /h/. Furthermore, notice that almost all of the weak forms are pronounced with a schwa.

This is the way native speakers talk, which is one of the reasons why Spanish students have difficulties in understanding properly as they cannot recognise words that they expect to be pronounced with their strong form: e.g. *You are* is not /ju: ɑ:/ but /jə ə/. In turn, Spanish people are not easily understood if they fail to take into account that any conversation in English is entirely based on connected speech.

For example, many Spanish speakers may mispronounce the sentence *How do you do?* by giving the same emphasis to the word *do*, which appears here twice, first as an auxiliary and then as an ordinary verb. Only the second one is stressed (pronounced /du:/), as it has a meaning, unlike the auxiliary verb (pronounced /də/), which only has a grammar function (it is used to form a question).

In summary, you should pronounce grammar words according to the weak forms. There are only a few exceptions. The only cases in which grammar words are pronounced with a strong form are:

- For emphasis: speakers can choose to stress grammar words to give them a special meaning. In written English, a word that is more important or emphasized than the others in a sentence is underlined or marked in *italics* or in **bold**. In spoken English, important words are distinguished through stress. Notice this in the conjunction of the sentence from Baker (2006, p. 148) *Put your head <u>and</u> heart into it*. The speaker emphasizes the grammar word to suggest a special meaning: *put not just your head, but also your heart,* so the pronunciation of *and* changes. When it is strongly stressed, *and* is pronounced /ænd/ (otherwise, it would usually be weak and pronounced /ənd/). Listen:

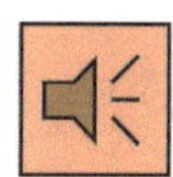

---

[1] Weak vowels: in almost all the cases, weakening is characterized by the replacement of a vowel phoneme by the shwa. Other weak vowels appearing in weak forms are /ɪ/ and /ʊ/.

*Pay attention: if you stress grammar words by mistake, it may cause a misunderstanding as the listener will look for a special meaning.

- To show contrast:

  The letter is <u>from</u> him, not <u>to</u> him (/ðə 'letə ɪz **frɒm** hɪm nɒt **tu:** hɪm/)

- At the end of a sentence:

  Weak: *I'm fond <u>of</u> chips* (/aɪm 'fɒnd əv 'ʧɪps/)
  Strong: *Chips are what I'm fond <u>of</u>* (/'ʧɪps ə 'wɒt aɪm 'fɒnd **ɒv**/)

- When verbs appear in final position, e.g., in short answers:

  Yes, you <u>could</u>. (/kʊd/)
  Has she been to the doctor? Yes, she's <u>been</u>. (/biːn/)

- When verbs appear in their negative form:

  aren't (/ɑːnt/); *can't* (/kɑːnt/); *don't* (/dəʊnt/) and *won't* (/wəʊnt/)

WEAK FORMS WITH TWO OPTIONS

These are some grammar words that are also pronounced in two different ways even in their weak form depending on the words/sounds that follow them in connected speech:

- *The:* the definite article is pronounced with schwa (/ðə/) if the following word starts with a consonant, and as /ðɪ/ if the following word starts with a vowel (e.g., *the egg* would be /ðɪ eg/).

- *A:* it is easier to remember the two variants of the indefinite article as it follows the same rule as in spelling (*a/an*). If the following word begins with a vowel sound (*an orange*), then the pronunciation is /ən/, but if the following word begins with a consonant sound (*a cat*), the pronunciation is /ə/.

- *And:* this conjunction is pronounced with /d/ at the end if the next word starts with a vowel and without /d/ if the following word starts with a consonant. For example, it is pronounced as /ən/ in *and me* but as /ənd/ in *and us*.

- *To:* this preposition is pronounced /tə/ only before consonants. If the next word begins with a vowel sound, then /tʊ/ is used. The same happens with /ɪntə/ and /ɪntʊ/.

- *You:* this pronoun is pronounced /jə/ before consonants and /jʊ/ before vowels.

- *There:* it is pronounced /ðə/ before consonants (*There were many people*), /ðər/ before vowels (*There are many people*) and /ðeə/ when it is an adverb of place (*It's there*).

- *That*: this is pronounced /ðət/ when it is a relative pronoun (*The thing that I told you about*) or a conjunction (*She said that he'd come*), but /ðæt/ when it is a demonstrative (*That is my car*).

WEAK FORMS LINKING

Finally, weak forms typically link with the surrounding words in natural speech. Notice how the unstressed words join with the words before and after them in the following examples from Hancock (2012, p. 102). The column on the right shows you a representation of how the unstressed words or syllables are all pronounced as if they were just one word:

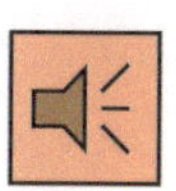

such an event	'such<u>an</u>event'
if I sing I mean	'<u>if</u>I sing<u>I</u> mean'
on the stage and you're doing	'on<u>the</u> stage<u>and</u>you're doing'
but I usually just try and	'but<u>I</u> usually just <u>tryand</u>'
and just kind of	'and just <u>kindof</u>'
and just go out and just do it	'<u>andjust</u> go <u>outand</u> just <u>doit</u>'

To progressively internalize the use of weak forms and acquire the skill of sounding more natural in conversation, shadowing is particularly useful. This is a well-known teaching practice in which "learners watch a short video multiple times, repeating after the speakers with the goal of precisely imitating the sounds, pauses, and intonation of their speech" (Yoshida 2018, p. 198). This is not an activity of mere repetition or imitation but a highly demanding cognitive task in which language is carefully scrutinized or analyzed, which increases phonetic awareness. Among others, you have to "remember speech input and reproduce it in real time. It requires [both] listening and speaking skills" (Sugiarto et al. 2020, p. 117).

II.   OTHER PHENOMENA OF CONNECTED SPEECH

1) **Linking r**: in British English /r/ is not pronounced when it appears in post-vocalic position or at the end of a word, e.g., *car*. However, this changes in connected speech: if the word that follows starts with a vowel we insert an /r/ there to link, e.g. *the car is blue*.

2) **Assimilation**: this happens when a sound becomes more phonetically similar to another due to their close proximity in connected speech, e.g.: *have to* (/hæv tuː/ → /hæf tuː/); *of course* (/əv kɔːs/ → /əf kɔːs/).

Listen to how the sounds at the end of a word acquire the quality of the sound at the beginning of the next word:

*Good girl. She's a goo**d** girl. ('goo<u>g</u> girl')* *
*Good boy. He's a goo**d** boy. ('goo<u>b</u> boy')*
*White paper. I only use whi**te** paper. ('whi<u>pe</u> paper')*
*Speed boat. I've never been in spee**d** boat. ('spee<u>b</u> boat')*
(examples from BBC Learning English)
*The sound at the end of the first word is taking the quality of the sound at the beginning of the second word. So the /d/ at the end of *good*, becomes like the /g/ at the start of *girl*.

3) **Elision**: this is when sounds disappear. When the sounds /t/ or /d/ occur between two consonant sounds, they will often disappear completely from the pronunciation:

*I'm going nex**(t)** week*
*That was the wors**(t)** job I ever had!*
*Jus**(t)** one person came to the party!*
*I can'**(t)** swim*
(examples from BBC Learning English)

4) **Sounds twinning** (gemination): when a word ends in a consonant sound and the following word begins with the same consonant sound, both sounds are pronounced together as one.

*I'm a bi**t t**ired*
*We have a lo**t t**o do*
*Tell me wha**t t**o say*
*She's slep**t f**or three hours*
I've finished
(examples from BBC Learning English)

EXERCICES: 

1-. Listen and repeat. Go to Youtube and look for the video "English Pronunciation Illustrated by John Trim" where you can find different phrases and sentences so that you can perceive and practice pronunciation in connected speech. Pauses are provided for repetition.

2-. Listen and write the words you hear. Then practice saying them.

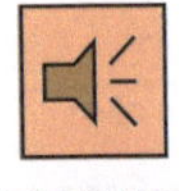

Can you tell her to call me, please?   *Where could ___ find ___ library?*
Can you give_____ to _____, please?   *What's ___ price of ____? Did _*
_____ meet_____ father?   *Where's _____ family ___?*
I don't think_____ remembers _____.   *_____ bought flowers for ___ teachers.*
Why did _____ lie to_____ ?

3-. In these sentences, both of the words underlined sound very similar in fast speech. Listen carefully and choose the word you hear:

I had a salad as/and a main course.
She sings a/the song.
Don't look at/for the man.
She showed me a vase of/for flowers.
Take some chocolates and/or pastries.
I like the/to cook.

4-. Transcribe the underlined words in their weak or strong forms:

What are you looking <u>at</u>? I am looking <u>at</u> her son.
<u>Does</u> anybody know where <u>that</u> thing over <u>there</u> came <u>from</u>?
What is <u>the</u> ugliest place <u>you have</u> ever been <u>to</u>?
<u>Have</u> you ever <u>had</u> to transcribe English words? Yes, I <u>have.</u>
The exercise <u>that</u> I gave <u>to</u> my students <u>wasn't</u> too difficult for <u>them</u>
<u>There</u> are no restaurants over there. Why <u>don't</u> we go to the other town?

5-. In the following sentences from Roach (2005, p. 109), the transcription for the weak form words (in bold) is left blank. Fill in the blanks, taking care to use the appropriate form (weak or strong):

*I want **her to** park that car over **there**.*
/aɪ wɒnt _______ pɑːk ðæt kɑːr ˈəʊvə _______ /

***Of** all **the** proposals, **the** one **that you** made **is** the silliest.*
/ __ ɔːl __ prəˈpəʊzəlz __ wʌn _______ meɪd ____ˈsɪlɪəst /

*Jane **and** Bill **could have** driven **them to and from the** party.*
/dʒeɪn __ bɪl _______ drɪvən _______________ ˈpɑːtɪ/

***To** come **to the** point, what **shall** we **do for the** rest **of the** week?*
/ __ kʌm _______ pɔɪnt wɒt _________ rest _______ wiːk/

***Has** anyone got **an** idea where it came **from**?*
/ __ ˈenɪwʌn gɒt __ aɪˈdɪə weər ɪt keɪm ____/

*Pedestrians **must** always use crossings provided **for them**.*
/pəˈdestriənz ____ ˈɔːlweɪz juːz ðə ˈkrɒsɪŋz prəˈvaɪdɪd_______/

*Each one **was a** perfect example **of the** art **that had been** developed **there**.*
/iːtʃ wʌn _______ ˈpɜːfekt ɪgˈzɑːmpəl ____ ɑːt _________ dɪˈveləpt _______ /

6-. Transcribe the following sentences and identify when the grammar words are transcribed either in their weak or strong form. Identify also the weak forms with two variants, morphemic "-s"/"-ed" and the presence of other speech phenomena.

I like to have tea with milk and sugar every morning.
The bull and the sheep eat leaves peacefully.
The cook listens to music while cooking a chicken soup.
The castle we visited in Austria was awesome.

7-. YouGlish (http://youglish.com/) is an exellent resource to know how individual words are pronounced in authentic discourse. For example, look for the phrase "it's a piece of cake" to watch videos using it in different and natural contexts. Remember that you can also filter by the accent that you prefer. Then choose a short video and practice shadowing: listen repeatedly by paying attention to its pronunciation features and imitate it until you can perfectly reproduce the original. Record yourself and compare your production with the video; you can use the available scripts to identify/analyze better the language used.

KEY

1. VOWELS

[Preliminary questions]

fish /fɪʃ/	sheep /ʃiːp/	cat /kæt/	hen /hen/
cockatoo /kɒkəˈtuː/	calf /kɑːf/	bull /bʊl/	/ bird /bɜːd/
duck /dʌk/	fox /fɒks/	horse /hɔːs/	gorilla /gəˈrɪlə/

Sound pair 1. SHIP OR SHEEP? Sounds /ɪ/ and /iː/

1-. /ɪ/: fish, chicken, insect, pig, iguana, giraffe
/iː/: zebra, sheep, beaver, peacock, cheetah, chimpanzee, seal

2-.

/ɪ/	/iː/
ship	sheep
hit	heat
live	leave
it	eat
bin	bean
fit	feet
tim	team

3-. piece; reach; peel; teach; people; need; these
4-. cheek; read; beat; mean; feel; bead
5-. still; these; bread
6-. live; lead; eat; sip

Sound pair 2. FULL OR FOOL? Sounds /ʊ/ and /u:/

1-. 2,1; 2,1; 1,2; 2,1; 2,1
2-. Lucy studied journalism at university in New York last fall. She had moved there for two months before summer, May and June, and then she looked for a beautiful apartment with a view. She used to go out for lunch in rooftops and try different food to amuse herself. Soon she knew that she was running out of money and she had to return to Europe. It was just too good to be true.
3-. You are not going to believe what happened to me at the swimming pool. I was trying to pull the door but it opened pushing.
Do you think she is such a fool that she forgot? No, I just think she is just full of problems to remember anything at all.
Luke was talking behind Lucy's back when I said 'Look! She's just there hearing everything.'
His suit was filthy because he had been trying to clean the soot.

4-.

/ u:/	/ʊ/
true	foot
toothbrush	good
soon	cook
lose	push
food	pull
	put
	could

Sound pair 3. SHOT OR SHORT? Sounds /ɒ/ and /ɔ:/

1-. 2,1; 1,2; 1,2; 1,2
2-. sports; pot; cord; shot; caller; caught

3-.

fog	RP	cough	RP
lodge	AE	cost	AE
not	AE	moth	RP
cod	RP	cross	AE
odd	AE	cloth	AE

Sound pair 4. HEAD OR HEARD? Sounds /e/ and /ɜ:/

1-. 1D, 2S, 3D, 4D, 5D, 6S, 7S
2-. turn; bent; worst; learnt
3-. bed; Bertie; lends; turn; west

Sound pair 5. CAT OR CUT? Sounds /æ/ and /ʌ/

1-.

/æ/	/ʌ/
bag	country
plan	number
jam	colour
bank	husband
traffic	butter
salad	mushroom
cabbage	pumpkin
carrot	cucumber

2-. cup; hut; bug; mud; hung; run; cut; but; begun: sung; truck; much; fun; mud; fush; bunker; flutter; buddie; crush; bung; bunk; rung; cub; dud; fund; rush; rug
3-. truck; hat; cup; cat; hang; run
4-. /æ/: salad, eggplant, cabbage, carrot, yam, asparagus
   /ʌ /: mushroom, pumpkin, cucumber
5-. January; father; ran; business; glad; word; push; common

Sound pair 6. HAT OR HEART? Sounds /æ/ and /ɑ:/

1-.

/æ/	/ɑ:/
cash	artist
jacket	garden
carry	class
factory	fast
camera	father

2-.

lark: /ɑ:/	lack: /æ/	luck: /ʌ/
bad: /æ/	bard: /ɑ:/	bud: /ʌ/
match: /æ/	much: /ʌ/	march: /ɑ:/
cart: /ɑ:/	cut: /ʌ/	cat: /æ/
cup: /ʌ/	carp: /ɑ:/	cap: /æ/
hut: /ʌ/	hat: /æ/	heart: /ɑ:/

3-. START

dark	drunk	watch	fan	can
smart	cat	starts	sunk	rabbit
class	half	can't	mother	staff
ham	jam	calm	father	dance
draw	bag	dare	man	card

END

4-. heart; cut; cap; barn; bud; back

THE SCHWA: Sound /ə/

1-. I come from London.
The brother was asleep.
The restaurant was open.
The doctor's assistant.
She answered the telephone.
A difficult question.

2-. address; away; teaches; drive; officer's; woman; driver's asleep

3-.

professor	remember
tomorrow	important
summer	readable
protect	about
wonderful	theatre
emotion	treas

4-. 1. It's a pres<u>e</u>nt <u>for you</u>.
    2. It takes <u>a</u> long time <u>to</u> get there.
    3. W<u>ould</u> <u>you</u> like <u>a</u> cup <u>of</u> tea?
    4. What <u>are</u> <u>you</u> doing t<u>o</u>night?
    5. What time will y<u>ou</u> arrive <u>at</u> th<u>e</u> stat<u>ion</u>?
    6. I h<u>ave</u> been studying English f<u>or</u> 5 years.
    7. Th<u>e</u> city cent<u>re</u> is closed <u>for a</u> demonstrat<u>ion</u>.
    8. Th<u>e</u> airport is rath<u>er</u> far fr<u>om</u> here.
    9. She works <u>as a</u> teach<u>er</u> and <u>as a</u> counse<u>lor</u> <u>for</u> th<u>e</u> gov<u>er</u>nment.
    10. We need s<u>o</u>me more help fr<u>om</u> th<u>e</u> lo<u>ca</u>l authorities.

2. CONSONANTS

[Preliminary questions]

parrot	bee	turtle	dog
/ˈpærət/	/biː/	/tɜːtəl/	/dɒg/
kangaroo	giraffe	fish	vulture
/kæŋgəˈruː/	/dʒɪˈrɑːf/	/fɪʃ/	/ˈvʌltʃə/
spider	zebra	shark	dressage
/spaɪdə/	/ˈzɪbrə/	/ʃɑːk/	/drəˈsɑːʒ/
moth	mother	chimpanzee	hedgehog
/mɒθ/	/ˈmʌðə/	/tʃɪmpænˈziː/	/ˈhedʒhɒg/
mouse	nightingale	monkey	hippo
/maʊs/	/ˈnaɪtɪŋgeɪl/	/mʌŋkɪ/	/ˈhɪpəʊ/
lion	rabbit	wolf	yak
/laɪən/	/rabɪt/	/wʊlf/	/jæk/

Sound pair 1. SEA OR SHE? Sounds /s/ and /ʃ/

1-. 1S, 2D, 3D, 4D, 5S, 6S, 7S
2-. so/<u>show</u>   seat/<u>sheet</u>   <u>suit</u>/shoot   <u>save</u>/shave   sign/<u>shine</u>   fist/<u>fished</u>

Sound pair 2. SUE OR ZOO? Sounds /s/ and /z/

1-. place/<u>plays</u>   Sue/<u>zoo</u>   <u>niece</u>/knees   piece/<u>peas</u>   pace/<u>pays</u>   ice/<u>eyes</u>
2-. You can have my tent. It's no <u>use</u> /s/to me. I never <u>use</u>/z/ it.
I'm not going to <u>advise</u> /z/ you. You never take my <u>advice</u>/s/. Your
tooth is <u>loose</u>/s/. You'll <u>lose</u>/z/ it if you're not careful.
The shop's very <u>close</u>/s/ to home, and it doesn't <u>close</u> /z/ till late. I
can't <u>excuse</u> /z/ people who drop litter. There's no <u>excuse</u>/s for it.
3-. price; he sat; shoot; saved

Sound pair 3. CHEAP OR JEEP? Sounds /ʧ/ and /ʤ/

1-.

/ʧ/	/ʤ/
teacher	lounge
chair	bridge
cicken	large
cheap	juice
dutch	language
chips	orange
cheese	dangerous

2-. guess; get, Christmas; give; picture

3-. /ʧ/: feature, children, temperatures, French
/ʤ/: gorgeous, Jardy, junior, management, jumping, staged, huge, enjoyed, Orangerie

Sound pair 4. MISSION OR VISION? Sounds /ʃ/ and /ʒ/

1-. /ʃ/: sugar /ˈʃʊgə/; machine /məˈʃiːn/; parachute /ˈpærəʃuːt/; brush /brʌʃ/
/ʒ/: vision /vɪʒən/; allusion /əˈluːʒən/; division /dɪˈvɪʒən/; measure /ˈmeʒə/; casual /kæʒuəl/; leisure /ˈleʒə/

2-.

/ʃ/	/ʒ/
Spanish	Russia
shake	pleasure
fashion	measure
shirt	casual
wash	revision
nation	
cash	
ocean	

3-.

	/ʃ/	/ʒ/
fish	X	
patient	X	
profession	X	
ambition	X	
exposure		X
beige		X
unusual		X
measure		X
devotion	X	
anxious	X	
illusion		X

4-. /ʃ/: competition, show, international, national, nations, option, spacious

Sound pair 5. LEAF OR LEAVE? Sounds /f/ and /v/

1-.

bet √	vet
best√	vest
bury	very√
by	vie√
bow√	vow
boat	vote√
bowel√	vowel
bent	vent√
ban	van√

2-.

proof	1	focal	2	half	2
prove	2	vocal	1	halve	1
fine	2	surf	1		
vine	1	serve	2		
grief	1	staff	1		
grieve	2	starve	2		
safe	2	leaf	1		
save	1	leave	2		

Sound pair 6. THREE OR THIS? Sounds /θ/ and /ð/

1-. /θ/: athletic /æθ'letɪk/; ethics /'eθɪks/; method /'meθəd/; author /'ɔ:θə/; mouth /maʊθ/
/ð/: gather /'gæðə/; although /ɔ:l'ðəʊ/; clothes /kləʊðz/

2-.

What are you <u>thinking</u> about?
I would like <u>another</u> coffee, please.
I am not very good at <u>maths.</u>
I'm looking for <u>the bathroom,</u> please.

Clean all <u>that</u> rubbish <u>thrown</u> over <u>there</u>?
My <u>teeth</u> are hurting.
Today is the <u>fourth</u> of July.
These clothes belong to my <u>mother</u>.

/θ/	/ð/
thinking	another
maths	the
bathroom	that; there
teeth	these; clothes; mother
fourth	
thrown	

3-. 1, 2, 2, 1, 2, 1, 2.

4-. Body parts (θ): mouth, tooth/teeth, thumb, throat, thigh
Time/Calendar (θ): Thursday, month, ordinal numbers three, thirteen and thirty, cardinal numbers third, fourth, twelfth, etc.
Proper names (θ): Ruth, Martha, Beth, Dorothy, Arthur, Theodore
Family/Kinship (ð): (grand)mother, (grand)father, stepmother, stepfather, sister (-in-law), brother (-in-law)
Pronouns (ð): they, them, this, these, that, those

Sound pair 7. YALE OR JAIL? Sounds /j/ and /dʒ/

1-.

your	2	yolk	1	yam	2
jaw	1	joke	2	jam	1
yak	2	year	1		
Jack	1	jeer	2		
Yale	1	yin	1		
Jail	2	gin	2		
you	2	yet	2		
Jew	1	jet	1		

2-. /j/: lawyer /ˈlɔːjə/; use /juːs/; muse /mjuːs/; education /edjuˈkeɪʃən/; avenue /ˈævənjuː/; argue /ˈɑːgjuː/; nephew /ˈnefjuː/ beauty /ˈbjuːtɪ/
/dʒ/: major /ˈmeɪdʒə/; magic /ˈmædʒɪk/; cage /keɪdʒ/; judge /dʒʌdʒ/; fridge /frɪdʒ/
3-. Yale; jokes; yes; years; juice; yob
4-. Jane can juggle jars.
Jim can do gymnastics.
John can jump joyfully, and James can jog largely on jagged hills.
What do you judge Jess and Jenny can generally do? They generously join Jazz.

Sound pair 8. RAN OR RANG? Sounds /n/ and /ŋ/

1-. 1D, 2S, 3D, 4S, 5S, 6S, 7D
2-. sinners; wing; bank; sung; thin; rank
rang; Ron; ban; sinking
3-. stronger; nothing; killing; stronger

Sound pair 9. GOOD OR WOULD? Sounds /g/ and /w/

1-. quick /kwɪk/; queen /kwiːn/; colloquial /kəˈləʊkwiəl/; adequate /ˈædɪkwət/; quality /ˈkwɒlətɪ/; language /ˈlæŋgwɪdʒ/; penguin /ˈpeŋgwɪn/; linguist /ˈlɪŋgwɪst/
2-. All of the words begin by /w/ except for whole: the initial sound is /h/ as "w" is silent.
All of the words begin by /w/ except for who: the initial sound is /h/ as "w" is silent.
All of the words begin by /w/ except for write: the initial sound is /r/ as "w" is silent.
3-.

How much wood would a woodchuck chuck if a woodchuck could chuck wood? He would chuck as much wood as a woodchuck could chuck.

4-. vine; veal; whale; invite; vet; worse
5-. wait; got; one; guy; wet; gone

Sound pair 10. EAR OR HEAR? Sound /h/

1-. hour & honest: /h/ is silent

2-.

tell her	/h/ in the pronoun is dropped: /ˈtel ə/
tell him	/h/ in the pronoun is dropped: /ˈtel ɪm/
ask her sister	/h/ in the pronoun is dropped: /ɑ:sk ə ˈsɪstə/
ask his sister	/h/ in the pronoun is dropped: /ɑ:sk ɪz ˈsɪstə/
her sister	/h/ in the pronoun is not dropped when at the beginning of a sentence: /ˈhə ˈsɪstə/
his sister	/h/ in the pronoun is not dropped when at the beginning of a sentence: /hɪz ˈsɪstə /

3-. old; hand; ill; heating; old; eight; heart

4-. eat; Helen; hold; hill; air; hate; art; hall; high

UK OR US ENGLISH? Sound /r/

1-.

word: AE	girl: RP
start: RP	teacher: RP
door: AE	calendar: RP
bird: RP	curl: AE
storm: AE	hammer: RP

3-.

1. The doctorX will arrive later√ on.
2. My father√ and my mother√ areX waiting for us.
3. AreX you far√ away from here?
4. Is there√ any sugar√ in the fridge?
5. The car√ is out of orderX.
6. You are√ as smart as yourX motherX.
7. The teacher√ and the students are√ in the History museum today.
8. There√ are more pencils overX there.
9. The letter√ arrived before√ I moved.
10. Our√ aunt always gives us a bar√ of chocolate.

3. MORPHEMIC RULES

I. "-ed" MORPHEME

1-.

(1) turned: /d/	(4) flicked: /t/	(7) wanted: /ɪd/	(10) headed: /ɪd/
(2) delayed: /d/	(5) waited: /ɪd/	(8) jumped: /t/	(11) tried: /d/
(3) browsed: /d/	(6) arrived: /d/	(9) dropped: /t/	(12) realised: /d/

2-. arrived; turned; rushed; replaced; equipped; marked; finished; allowed; switched; designed

3-. walked; want; play; danced; call; helped; enjoy; followed

5-. finished; asked; added; liked, lasted; watch; walked; show; pass

6-. 

II. "-s" MORPHEME

1-. meets; plays; teaches; pets; faces; wives; notebooks; plates; animals; provides
2-. scarves; knives; thief's; halves; wife's; life's; calf's
3-. /s/: gets; walks; waits; gets; walks; sits; sits; walks; thinks; gets, eats; thinks; gets; waits
/z/: Mondays; Fridays; has; comes; Saturdays; Sundays; does; goes; comes; goes; goes;
doesn't; doesn't; stays; does
/ɪz/: watches; watches

4-.

	/s/	/z/	/ɪz/
plurals	weeks	eggs	wages
present simple	drinks	wins	watches
possessive	Mark's	Tom's	Rose's
is/has contractions	it's	he's	

5-. START

clocks	drinks	moves	dolls	washes
gloves	shops	starts	sinks	rabbits
plays	kisses	clowns	cars	months
feels	roses	comes	girls	jokes
draws	boxes	dares	beers	books

END

6-. - judges /ˈdʒʌdʒɪz/; lives /lɪvz/; plates /pleɪts/; classes /ˈklɑːsɪz/; breathes /briːðz/;
watches /ˈwɒtʃɪz/; attends /əˈtendz/; tapes /teɪps/; books /bʊks/; wives /waɪvz/
- shines /ʃaɪnz/; rays /reɪz/; rocks /rɒks/; eggs /egz/; orders /ˈɔːdəz/; churches /ˈtʃɜːtʃɪz/;
puts /pʊts/; watches /ˈwɒtʃɪz/; manages /ˈmænɪdʒɪz/; hours /ˈaʊəz/
- buses /ˈbʌsɪz/; goes /gəʊz/; cows /kaʊz/; steaks /steɪks/; hates /heɪts/; pitches /ˈpɪtʃɪz/;
bushes /ˈbʊʃɪz/; laughs /lɑːfs/; stores /stɔːz/; rings /rɪŋz/

7-. *Jim speaks three languages*: /dʒɪm spiːks θriː ˈlæŋgwɪdʒɪz/
"Speaks": the third person form of the present simple verb is pronounced as /s/ because
the last sound in the infinitive (*speak*) is voiceless (/k/)
"Languages": here we have to consider the last sound of the singular word, which is the
sibilant /dʒ/, therefore the corresponding pronunciation of the plural form is /ɪz/.

Here is a reminder of the RULE for the plural or 3rd person "-s" in the present simple:
You always need to consider the last sound in the singular or in the infinitive of the verb:
1. If the sound is voiceless (/p, t, k, ʧ, f, θ, s, ʃ, h/), we add /s/
2. If the sound is voiced (/b, d, g, ʤ, v, ð, z, ʒ, m, n, ŋ, l, r, j, w/ + VOWELS + DIPTHONGS), we add /z/
3. If the last sound is a sibilant: (/s, z, ʃ, ʒ, ʧ, dʒ/), we add /ɪz/

4. STRESS

1-.

O	oO	oOo	oOoo	Ooo
cut	*explain*	*amazing*	*imposible*	*suitable*
/pliːz/	/bɪˈgɪn/	/dɪˈrɛkʃən/	/inˈkredəbl/	/ˈfɜːnɪtʃə/
/klɪə/	/əkˈsept/	/riˈmembə/	/ɪn ˈtenʃənl/	/ˈenɪwʌn/
/bæŋk/	/əˈbʌv/	/nəˈvembə/		/ˈjestədi/
	/kəˈlekc	/təˈmɒrəu/		/ˈbjuːtɪfʊl/

2-. Texas; Japan; politics; computer; impossible

3-. Fish B is caught. The sentences or phrases are matched as follows:
- Look = Wait.
- Begin! = She talked.
- Who cares? = Don't stop!
- Don't worry! = Keep quiet!
- They've arrived. = I insist.
- They've finished. = I've seen it.
- What's the time? = Don't forget!
- See you later! = Come and see us!
- I spoke to John. = He wants to come.
- Where was he from? = What do you want?
- She tried to call you. = I can't believe it.

4-.

OooO	oOoO	OoO	OoOo
What do you think?	The train was late.	Come and try.	Close the window.
Give me a chance.	The water's hot.	Where's the car?	Nice to meet you.
What did she say?	It's cold and wet.	What's the time?	Phone and tell me.

5-. <u>Get</u> the <u>strangers</u>
out of our <u>house</u>!
<u>That</u>,
believe it or not,
is how my <u>grandmother</u>
would <u>greet</u> my friends.
As you can <u>imagine</u>,
I wasn't really <u>fond</u> of her.
This is a <u>photo</u> of my <u>grandmother</u>,
on her <u>fourth</u> <u>birthday</u>
in <u>1909</u> in <u>New York City</u>.
When I was <u>16</u>,

I found out that the <u>day</u> after this <u>picture</u> was taken,
she was <u>kidnapped</u>,
<u>abducted</u> by one of the <u>gangs</u> of <u>extortionists</u>
known as the <u>Black Hand</u> that <u>pried</u> on <u>Little Italies</u>.
They had her <u>3 months</u>
and it was <u>only</u> because of the <u>strength</u>
and <u>cunning</u>
of my great-grandmother
that she was <u>returned</u> to life.
It took me <u>years</u> to get the <u>full story</u>,
but when I <u>did</u>
I was <u>finally</u> able to <u>love my grandmother</u>
<u>and</u> to <u>understand</u>
the <u>transformative power</u> of
knowing you <u>family history</u>.

5. CONNECTED SPEECH

2-. it, us; he, our; he, her; you, them; we, a; the, this; her, from; we, the
3-. as; a; for; of; and; to
4-. What are you looking <u>at</u>? I am looking <u>at</u> her son.
                                   /æt/   /ət/
<u>Does</u> anybody know where <u>that</u> thing over <u>there</u> came <u>from</u>?
/dəz/   /ðæt/   /ðeə/   /frɒm/
     What is <u>the</u> ugliest place <u>you</u> <u>have</u> ever been <u>to</u>?
                     /ðɪ/   /jə/ /həv/   /tuː/
<u>Have</u> you ever <u>had</u> to transcribe English words? Yes, I <u>have</u>
/həv/   /hæd/   /hæv/
<u>The</u> exercise <u>that</u> I gave <u>to</u> my students <u>wasn't</u> too difficult for <u>them</u>.
ðɪ   ðət   tə   ˈwɒznt   /ðəm/
<u>There</u> are no restaurants over there. Why <u>don't</u> we go to the other town?
/ðər/   /dəʊnt/
5-. I want **her to** park that car over **there**.
/aɪ wɒnt (h)ə tə pɑːk ðæt kɑːr ˈəʊvə ðeə/
Of all **the** proposals, **the** one **that you** made **is** the silliest.
/ əv ɔːl ðə prəˈpəʊzəlz ðə wʌn ðət jə meɪd ɪz ðə ˈsɪlɪəst /
Jane **and Bill could have** driven **them to and from the** party.
/dʒeɪn ən bɪl kəd həv drɪvən ðəm tuː ən frɒm ðə ˈpɑːtɪ/
To come **to the** point, what **shall** we **do for the** rest **of the** week?
/tə kʌm tə ðə pɔɪnt wɒt ʃəl wɪ duːfə ðə rest əv ðə wiːk/
Has anyone got **an** idea where it came **from**?
/həz ˈeniwʌn gɒt ən aɪˈdɪə weər ɪt keɪm frɒm/
Pedestrians **must** always use crossings provided **for them**.
/pəˈdestriənz məst ˈɔːlweɪz juːz ðə ˈkrɒsɪŋz prəˈvaɪdɪd fə ðəm/

Each one **was a** perfect example **of the** art that **had been** developed **there**.
/iːtʃ wʌn wəz əˈpɜːfekt ɪgˈzɑːmpəl əv ðɪ ɑːt ðət həd biːn dɪˈveləpt ðeə /
6-. I like to have tea with milk and sugar every morning:
     /aɪ laɪk **tə hæv** tiː wɪð mɪlk **ən** ˈʃʊgər ˈevrɪ ˈmɔːnɪŋ/

- "To" is a grammatical word (auxiliaries, prepositions, articles, conjunctions) and except in final position, it is transcribed with /ə/. In final position, it is emphasised and in that case it would be transcribed with /u:/.
- "Have" is here a lexical verb rather than an auxiliary (e.g. in *Have you taken the test?*, *have* is the auxiliary, and *take* is the lexical or main verb of the sentence). As a lexical verb, *have* is transcribed with /æ/; as an auxiliary, it would be transcribed with schwa /ə/.
- "And" is a conjunction and, therefore, a grammatical word. as such, it is transcribed with schwa //ə/ and without /d/ if a consonant follows, as in this case, or with /d/, as /ənd/, if a vowel follows.
- Remember that in British English we would not pronounce an /r/ at the end of the word "sugar". However, the word that follows starts with a vowel and we insert an /r/there to link. This is called a "linking r" and we always have it when a word ends in schwa /ə/ and the next one starts with a vowel, as in this case.

> *The bull and the sheep eat leaves peacefully:*
> /ðə bʊl ən ðə ʃi:p i:t **li:vz** ˈpi:sfʊlɪ/

- "The": the article is a grammatical word, like prepositions, articles, auxiliaries, and conjunctions (nouns, verbs and adjectives are lexical words). "The" is transcribed with schwa /ə/.
- "And": remember that this conjunction is transcribed with /d/ if the next word starts with a vowel and without /d/ if the following word starts with a consonant. In this case, the following word starts with a consonant /ðə/, and this is why we transcribe "and" as /ən/ here.
- "The": the article is transcribed with schwa if the following word starts with a consonant, and as /ði/ if the following word starts with a vowel (e.g., *the egg* would be /ði eg/).
- "Leaves" is an irregular plural (*leaf-leaves*) and it is transcribed as /li:vz/.

> *The cook listens to music while cooking a chicken soup:*
> /ðə kʊk ˈlɪsənz tə ˈmju:zɪk waɪl ˈkʊkɪŋ ə ˈtʃɪkɪn su:p/

- "The": "the" is transcribed with schwa /ə/ here because the following word starts with a consonant, rather than with a vowel.
- "Listens": the last phoneme in the infinitive /n/ is voiced, so the morphemic "-s" is pronounced as /z/.
- "To": the preposition is a grammatical word and as such, it is usually transcribed with schwa /tə/, unless emphasised for a specific purpose.

> *The castle we visited in Austria was awesome:*
> /ðə ˈka:səl wɪ ˈvɪzɪtɪd ɪn ˈɒstrɪə wəz ˈɔ:səm/

- "The": this article is a weak form → /ðə/ (when followed by word starting with consonant).
- "We": the pronoun is also a weak form → /wɪ/ (with the short vowel).
- "Visited": to know how to pronounce the "-ed" ending, we have to consider the last sound in the infinitive. In this case, it is a /t/, and when the last phoneme is /t/ or /d/, we add /ɪd/.
- "Was": the verb *to be*, when it is both a lexical verb and an auxiliary, is usually pronounced with a schwa → /wəz/ (unless it is emphasized or appears in final position of a sentence).

BIBLIOGRAPHY

Baker, A. (2003). *Sheep or Ship*. Cambridge: Cambridge University Press.

Bobkina, J., y De Caleya, M.F. (2010). *Fonética inglesa práctica: Manual didáctico para el profesorado*. CCS.

Bowler, B. (2005). *Timesaver Pronunciation Activities*. Mary Glasgow.

Calvo-Benzies, Y.J. (2017). "Contributions of New Technologies to the Teaching of English Pronunciation". *Language Value* 9.1.

Calvo-Benzies, Y.J. (2016). *The Teaching and Learning of English Pronunciation in Spain. An Analysis and Appraisal of Students' and Teachers' Views and Teaching Materials*. PhD dissertation. Santiago: Universidad de Santiago de Compostela.

Calvo Benzies Y.J. (2013) "Advanced Spanish university students problems with the pronunciationof English vowels. Identification, analysis and teaching implications". *ODISEA* 14: 37-56.

Celce-Murcia, M. (1983). "Teaching Pronunciation Communicatively". *Mextesol Journal* 7.1: 10-25.

Celce-Murcia, M., Brinton, D., y Ann Snow, M. (2014). *Teaching English as a Second or Foreign Language*. Boston: National Geographic Learning.

Celce-Murcia, M., Brinton, y D. Goodwin, J. (1996). *Teaching Pronunciation: A Referecee for Teachers of English to Speakers of Other Languages*. Cambridge: Cambridge University Press.

Celce-Murcia, M., Brinton, D., Goodwin, J., y Griner, B. (2010). *Teaching Pronunciation: A Course Book and Reference Guide*. Cambridge: Cambridge University Press.

Derwing, T.M., y Munro, M.J. (2005). "Second language accent and pronunciation teaching: A research-based approach". *TESOL Quarterly* 39.3: 379-397.

Estebas Vilaplana, E. (2009). *Teach Yourself English Pronunciation: An Interactive course for Spanish speakers*. Madrid, UNED.

Estebas Vilaplana, E. (2019). *Teach Yourself English Phonetics*. Madrid, UNED.

Finch, D., y Ortiz Lira, H. (1982). *A Course in English Phonetics for Spanish Speakers*. London, Heinemann Educational Books.

Hancock, M. (1995). *Pronunciation Games*. Cambridge: Cambridge University Press.

Hancock, M. (2012). *English Pronunciation in Use: Intermediate*. Cambridge, Cambridge University Press.

Harmer, J. (2001). *The Practice of English Language Teaching*. Longman.

Hewings, M. (2004). *Pronunciation Practice Activities: A Resource Book for Teaching English Pronunciation*. New York, Cambridge University Press.

Isaacs, T., y Trofimovich, P., eds. (2016). *Second Language Pronunciation Assessment: Interdisciplinary Perspectives*. Multilingual Matters.

Jones, R.H. (1997). "Beyond 'Listen and repeat': Pronunciation Teaching Materials and Theories of Second Language Acquisition". *System* 25.1: 103-112.

Kelly, G. (2000). *How To Teach Pronunciation.* Longman.

Kenworthy, J. (1989). *Teaching English Pronunciation.* Harlow, Longman.

Kirkova-Naskova, A., Henderson, A., y Fouz-González, J. (2020). *English Pronunciation Instruction: Research-based Insights.* Amsterdam: John Benjamins.

Levis, J.M. (2006). "Pronunciation and the Assessment of Spoken Language." Spoken English, *TESOL and applied linguistics.* London: Palgrave Macmillan. 245-270.

Llisterri, J. (200). "Enseñanza de la pronunciación, corrección fonética y nuevas tecnologías". *Es Espasa, Revista de Profesores* 28: 1-35.

Marks, J. (2003). *English Pronunciation in Use: Elementary,* Cambridge, Cambridge University Press.

Morley, J. (1991). "The Pronunciation Component in Teaching English to Speakers of Other Languages". *TESOL Quarterly* 25.3: 481-520.

Nunan, D. (2015) *Teaching English to speakers of other languages: An introduction.* London: Routledge.

Oxenden, C., Latham-Koenig, C., y Seligson, P. (2004). *New English File: Elementary Student's Book.* Oxford, Oxford University Press.

Ragusa, K. (2006). *The Skin Between Us: A Memoir of Race, Beauty, and Belonging.* WW Norton & Company.

Roach, P. (2005). *English Phonetics and Phonology.* Cambridge, Cambridge University Press.

Sugiarto, Rio, Prihantoro, P., y Edy, S. (2020). "The Impact of Shadowing Technique on Tertiary Students' English Pronunciation". *Linguists: Journal of Linguistics and Language Teaching* 6.1: 114-125.

Trim, J. (2001). *English Pronunciation Illustrated.* Cambridge, Cambridge University Press.

Wells, J. (2008). *Longman Pronunciation Dictionary.* Longman.

Webgraphy

Rachel's English (Videos)

   https://rachelsenglish.com

BBC Learning English (Pronunciation)

   https://www.bbc.co.uk/worldservice/learningenglish/grammar/pron/

   https://www.bbc.co.uk/worldservice/learningenglish/grammar/pron/sounds/

English with Lucy (Pronunciation)

   https://www.youtube.com/   EnglishwithLucy

Liveworksheets (Activities)

   https://www.liveworksheets.com/worksheets?keys=pronunciation&age=

ANNEXES

Annex 1: Sound Bank

VOWELS

PHONEME/SOUND	GRAPHEME/SPELLING	EXAMPLES
/æ/	"a"	cat
/ʌ/	"u"	sun
	"o"	son
	"ou"	young
	"oe"	does
/ɑ:/	"a"	ask
	"ar"	car
	"an"	dance
	"al"	calm
	"au"	laugh
	"ear"	heart
/e/	"e"	dress
	"ea"	head
	"ai"	again
	"ay"	says
	"ie"	friend
	"a"	any
	"u"	bury
/ɜ:/	"er"	perfect
	"ear"	earl
	"ir"	bird,
	"or"	work,
	"ur"	church
	"our"	journey
/ɪ/	"i"	ticket
	"y"	happy
/i:/	"ee"	tree
	"ea"	tea
	"ie"	piece
	"ei"	ceiling
/ɒ/	"o"	shop
	"a"	what
	"au"	because
/ɔ:/	"or"	horse
	"oor"	door
	"ore"	more
	"our"	four
	"ough"	bought
	"augh"	daughter
	"au"	author
	"ar"	war
	"al"	talk
	"aw"	law
/ʊ/	"u"	put

	"oo"	*food*
/u:/	"ou"	*group*
	"ue"	*blue*
	"ui"	*fruit*
	"o"	*move*
	"u"	*june*
	"ew"	*new*
	"a"	*alone*
	"e"	*broken*
/ə/	"i"	*impossible*
	"o"	*produce*
	"u"	*suspect*

CONSONANTS

PHONEME/SOUND	GRAPHEME/SPELLING	EXAMPLES
/p/	"p"	*pea*
	"gh"	*hiccough*
/b/	"b"	*book*
/t/	"t"	*tea*
	"th"	*thyme*
	"-ed"	*looked*
	"ght"	*eight*
/d/	"d"	*dog*
	"-ed"	*earned*
/k/	"k"	*key*
	"c"	*car*
	"ck"	*dock*
	"ch"	*school*
	"qu"	*queue*
	"x"	*explanation*
/g/	"g"	*give*
	"gh"	*ghost*
	"gu"	*guest*
/tʃ/	"ch"	*church*
	"tch"	*fetch*
	"t"	*nature*
	"c"	*cello*
/dʒ/	"j"	*jump*
	"dg"	*hedge*
	"g"	*large*
	"ch"	*sandwich*
/f/	"f"	*four*
	"ph"	*phone*
/v/	"v"	*veal*
/θ/	"th"	*thin*
/ð/	"th"	*the*

/s/	"s"	*see*
	"c"	*cinema*
	"z"	*eczema*
/z/	"z"	*zoo*
	"s"	*phrase*
	"ss"	*dessert*
	"x"	*exam*
/r/	"r"	*red*
/ʃ/	"sh"	*she*
	"c"+sion	*expulsion*
	"tion"	*caution*
	"sch"	*schwa*
	"ch"	*champagne*
/ʒ/	"v"+sion	*confusion*
	"v"+sure	*closure*
	"v"+sual	*casual*
	"g"	*genre*
/r/	"r"	*red*
/h/	"h"	*he*
	"wh"	*who*
/l/	"l"	*lake*
	"ll"	*umbrella*
/m/	"m"	*mother*
/n/	"n"	*nose*
/ŋ/	"n"	*think*
/w/	"w"	*wild*
	"wh"	*white*
	"u"	*quite*
	"oi"	*choir*
	"o"	*one*
/j/	"y"	*yoke*
	"u"	*music*

Annex 2: Symbols of English Sounds

INTERNATIONAL PHONETIC ALPHABET

/ɪ/ fil	/iː/ feel	/ʊ/ cook	/uː/ moon
/æ/ map	/ʌ/ bus	/ɑː/ car	/ə/ mother
/e/ pet	/ɜː/ girl	/ɒ/ clock	/ɔː/ door

Vowel sounds of English (phonetic symbols)

/p/ pot	/t/ tea	/k/ king
/b/ ball	/d/ day	/g/ gate
/f/ few	/v/ vote	/θ/ Thursday
/ð/ they	/s/ sing	/z/ zebra
/ʃ/ she	/ʒ/ pleasure	/tʃ/ chess
/dʒ/ Jhon	/l/ lake	/r/ red
/m/ Monday	/n/ new	/ŋ/ think
/h/ hair	/j/ you	/w/ wind

Consonant sounds of English (phonetic symbols)

Annex 3: Speech Organs

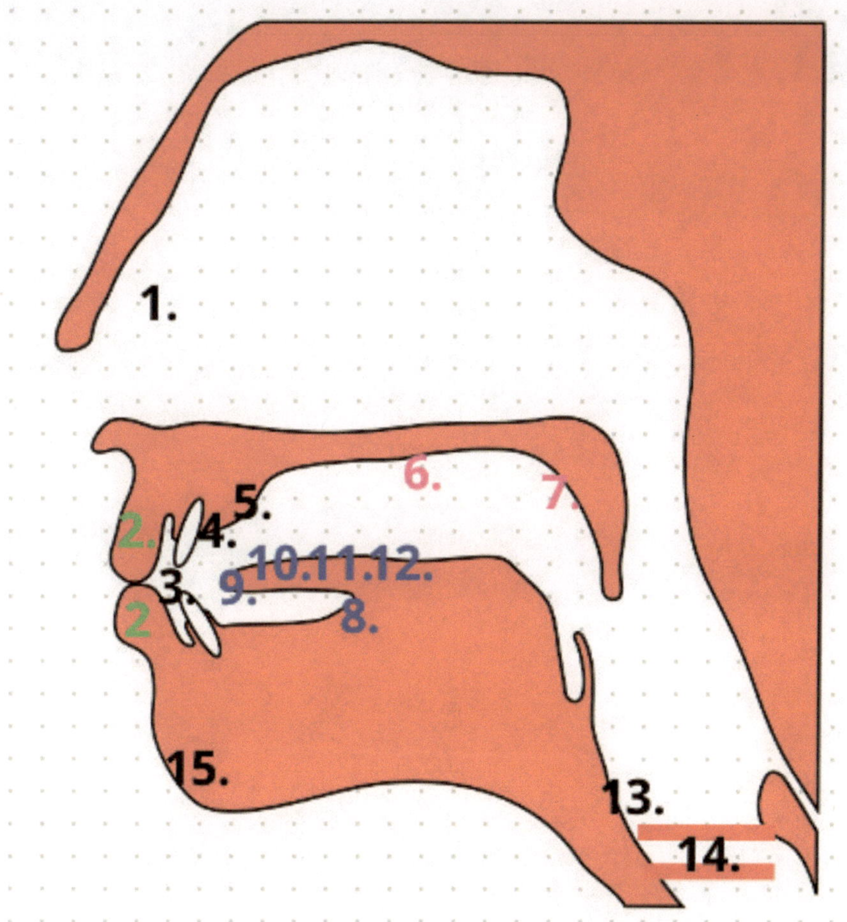

1. Nasal cavity (nasal sounds)
2. Lip (upper/low) (bilabial and labiodental sounds)
3. Teeth (dental and labiodental sounds)
4. Alveolar ridge (alveolar sounds)
5. Postalveolar
6. Hard palate (palatal sounds)
7. Soft palate or velum (velar sounds)

8. Tongue
9. Tip of the tongue
10. Blade of the tongue
11. Front of the tongue
12. Back of the tongue
13. Larynx
14. Vocal cords

Classification of the English consonants according to their <u>*Place of articulation*</u> *(1-9).*

<u>*Speech Organs*</u> *involved in the production of each consonant.*

Annex 4: Weak Forms

AUXILIARY VERBS
BE (am, are, is, was, were, been)
DO (does)
HAVE (have, has, had)
CAN (could)
WOULD
SHOULD
WILL
MUST

PRONOUNS
YOU (your)
HE (his, him)
SHE (her)
WE (us)
them
me

PREPOSITIONS
AS
AT
FOR
FROM
OF
TO

CONJUNCTIONS
AND
AS
BUT
THAN
THAT
OR

ARTICLES
A
AN
THE

INDEFINITE ADJECTIVES
ANY
SOME
SUCH

Annex 5: Further Pronunciation Resources

USEFUL VIDEO LESSONS

Sounds of English Vowels and Consonants with Phonetic symbols

International Phonetic Alphabet (IPA)

BOX SET: The complete guide to English Pronunciation. Learn ALL 44 sounds of English

The Schwa (/ə/): How to Pronounce the Schwa in English

Syllables and Word Stress

Sentence Stress

Weak Forms: How to Pronounce Weak Forms in English

Rhythm and Connected Speech

Annex 6: Extra Exercices: Pairwork/Role-Play

In pairs, work with a partner (the waiter) to order some food in a restaurant from the menu below. Make sure to pronounce each word with the appropriate sound: /ɪ/ or /iː/. Use a dictionary if necessary. You can use the following prompts to ask and answer questions in the conversation:

- *What would you like for first/main course?*

- *What will you have to drink?*

- *Which vegetable/side dish?*

- *And for dessert?*

Annex 7: Interactive Exercices

Sample of online exercices which allow students to learn or practice English pronunciation in an interactive and autonomous way (extracted from *Liveworksheet*s). This sample is organized according to different features of English pronunciation covered in the Manual. Access to the original source is given throuh the QR. Students are recommended to look for other activities depending on their particular needs.

POINT OF ARTICULATION/SPEECH ORGANS

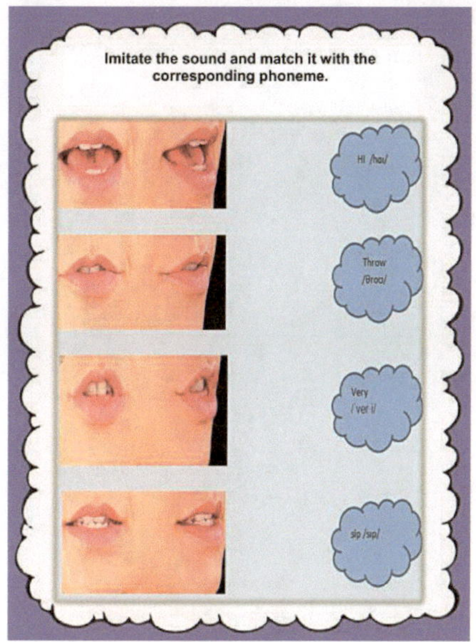

INTERNATIONAL PHONETIC ALPHABET (IPA)

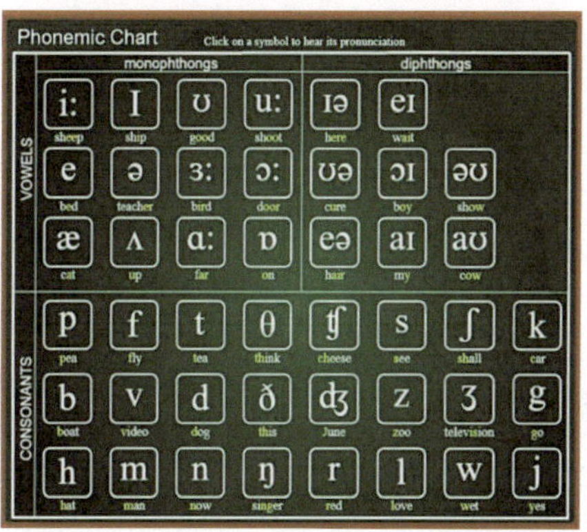

(INVERSE) TRANSCRIPTION

Phonetic Transcription – Clothes

How are the given words spelled correctly? Write them into the gaps.

1. ˈdʒækɪt →
2. ʃɜːt →
3. blaʊz →
4. kæp →
5. dʒiːnz →
6. skɑːf →
7. ˈtreɪnəz →
8. skɜːt →
9. ˈswetə →
10. ˈkəʊt →

Phonetic Transcription – Colours

1. griːn →
2. gəʊld →
3. bluː →
4. blæk →
5. ˈɒrɪndʒ →
6. braʊn →
7. ˈjeləʊ →
8. greɪ →
9. ˈpɜːpl →
10. waɪt →

Write the transcribed words on the left with ordinary letters.

e.g.	Chair	/tʃeə/
1		/ˈtiːtʃə/
2		/ bʊk/
3		/ pen/
4		/ dɔːg/
5		/ˈmʌndeɪ/
6		/ həˈləʊ/
7		/ˈrʌʃə/
8		/ əˈmerəkən/
9		/ mjuːˈzɪʃən/
10		/ˈlɔːjə/
11		/ˈmærid/
12		/ əˈdres/
13		/ˈstjuːdənt/
14		/ˈfraɪdeɪ/
15		/ juːnəˈvɜːsəti/
16		/ˈtjuːzdeɪ/
17		/ gɜːl/
18		/ˈdʒɜːmən/
19		/ ɪnˈdʒɔɪ/
20		/ˈtʃɪldrən/
21		/ nɜːs/
22		/ frentʃ/
23		/ˈtʃɒklət/
24		/ˈbɒtl/
25		/ aɪ ˈjuːʒəli duː maɪ ˈhəʊmwɜːk ət naɪt/

Translate these phonetic sentences into written English sentences.

ðə ˈlaɪən ænd ðə ˈræbɪt.

ə ˈkruːəl ˈlaɪən lɪvd ɪn ðə ˈfɒrəst.

ˈɛvəri deɪ, hi kɪld ænd eɪt ə lɒt ʌv ˈænɪməlz.

ðɪ ˈʌðər ˈænɪməlz wɜr əˈfreɪd ðə ˈlaɪən wʊd kɪl ðɛm ɔl.

ðɪ ˈænəməlz təʊld ðə ˈlaɪən,

"lɛts meɪk ə dil. ɪf ju ˈprɒmɪs tu it ˈəʊnli wʌn ˈænɪməl iːʧ deɪ,

ðɛn wʌn ʌv ʌs wɪl kʌm tu ju ˈɛvəri deɪ. ðɛn ju dəʊnt hæv tu hʌnt ænd kɪl ʌs."

ðə plæn ˈsaʊndəd wɛl θɔt-aʊt tu ðə ˈlaɪən, səʊ hi əˈgrid, bʌt hi ˈɔlsəʊ sɛd,

Reading transcriptions: listen, read and record.

❖ TOUCH ON THE WORD TO LISTEN

❖ TOUCH ON THE 🎤 MIC TO RECORD YOUR VOICE

/laɪt/	light	
/θɔːt/	thought	
/hɛd/	head	
/ˈʌndə/	under	
/ˈstɔːri/	story	
/sɔː/	saw	
/lɛft/	left	
/dəʊnt/	don't	
/fjuː/	few	
/waɪl/	while	
/əˈlɒŋ/	along	
/maɪt/	might	
/ˈkləʊs/	close	
/ˈsʌmθɪŋ/	something	
/siːm/	seem	
/nɛkst/	next	
/hɑːd/	hard	
/ˈəʊpən/	open	
/ɪgˈzɑːmpl/	example	
/bɪˈgɪn/	begin	

VOWELS

Short and long vowel sounds

Iː READ	I SIT	ʊ BOOK	uː TOO
e MEN	ə AMERICA	ɜː WORD	ɔː SORT
æ CAT	ʌ BUT	ɑː PART	ɒ HOT

LISTEN TO EACH WORD. CHOOSE THE CORRECT VOWEL SOUND.

CLOCK / STOP — ɒ ɔː

SLIPPED / BIN — Iː I

STAND / HAND — ʌ ɑː æ

BUTTER / UNDER — ʌ ɑː æ

SEEM / MEAN — Iː I

TEST / GUESS — e ɜː

BOUGHT / CAUGHT — ɒ ɔː

COULD / FOOT — ʊ uː

GIRL / DIRT — e ɜː

RUDE / TOOL — ʊ uː

HEART / PART — ʌ ɑː æ

Practicing sounds through tongue twisters: listen and record.

Listen to the audio and use the microphone button to record the tongue twister for each sentence.

🔊 FOUR FURIOUS FRIENDS FOUGHT FOR THE PHONE.

🔊 BETTY'S BIG BUNNY BOBBLED BY THE BLUEBERRY BUSH.

🔊 SHE SELLS SEASHELLS BY THE SEASHORE.

🔊 SUSIE WORKS IN A SHOE SHINE SHOP.

🔊 A BIG BLACK BAT IN A BIG BLACK BACKPACK.

🔊 A SNAKE SNEAKS TO SEEK A SNACK.

🔊 I SCREAM YOU SCREAM WE ALL SCREAM FOR ICE CREAM.

CONSONANTS

Discriminating two similar sounds (Pairs): watch, listen and repeat.

Silent letters

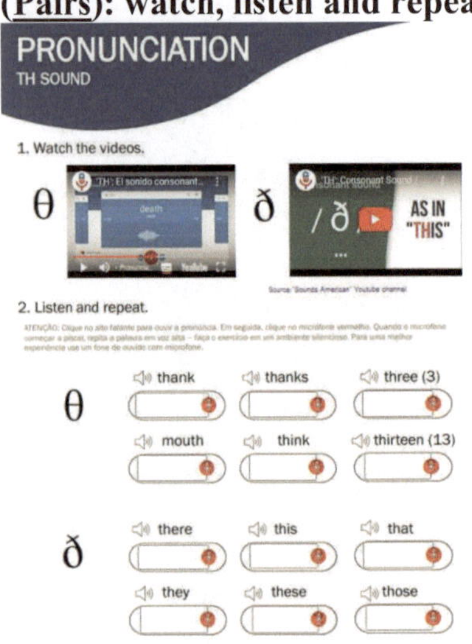

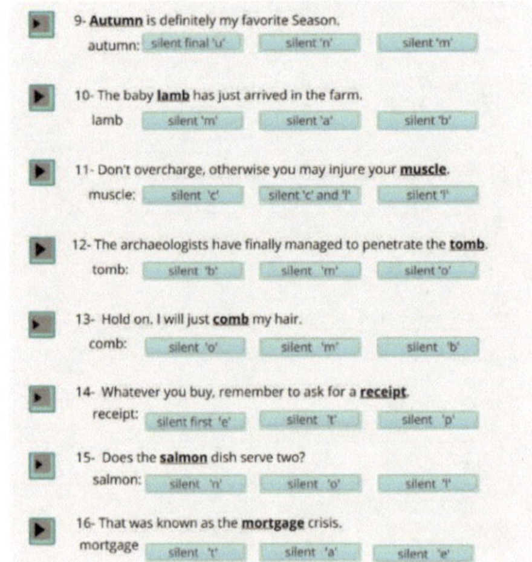

9- **Autumn** is definitely my favorite Season.
autumn: silent final 'u' | silent 'n' | silent 'm'

10- The baby **lamb** has just arrived in the farm.
lamb: silent 'm' | silent 'a' | silent 'b'

11- Don't overcharge, otherwise you may injure your **muscle**.
muscle: silent 'c' | silent 'c' and 'l' | silent 'l'

12- The archaeologists have finally managed to penetrate the **tomb**.
tomb: silent 'b' | silent 'm' | silent 'o'

13- Hold on, I will just **comb** my hair.
comb: silent 'o' | silent 'm' | silent 'b'

14- Whatever you buy, remember to ask for a **receipt**.
receipt: silent first 'e' | silent 't' | silent 'p'

15- Does the **salmon** dish serve two?
salmon: silent 'n' | silent 'o' | silent 'l'

16- That was known as the **mortgage** crisis.
mortgage: silent 't' | silent 'a' | silent 'e'

MORPHEMIC RULES

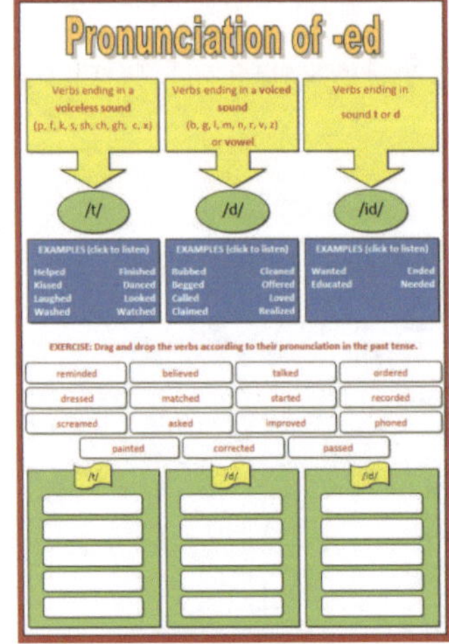

Listen to the sentences and choose the correct option in parentheses.

1. My parents (asked / ask) me many questions about the exam.
2. The teachers (explained / explain) the homework.
3. A lot of people (called / call) me for my birthday.
4. Firemen (helped / help) people in danger.
5. Lucy and Peter (invented / invent) a new game.
6. My brothers (played / play) basketball very well.
7. My friends (started / start) a new hobby.
8. The children (listened / listen) to the story.

Listen and record the correct pronunciation.

VERB – BASE FORM	VERB: PAST TENSE
• WATCH	• WATCH**ED** /t/
• LISTEN	• LISTEN**ED** /d/
• SHOUT	• SHOUT**ED** /id/
• CARRY	• CARRI**ED** /d/
• LOCK	• LOCK**ED** /t/
• START	• START**ED** /id/
• LIKE	• LIKE**D** /t/
• NOTICE	• NOTIC**ED** /d/
• TALK	• TALK**ED** /t/
• WANT	• WANT**ED** /id/

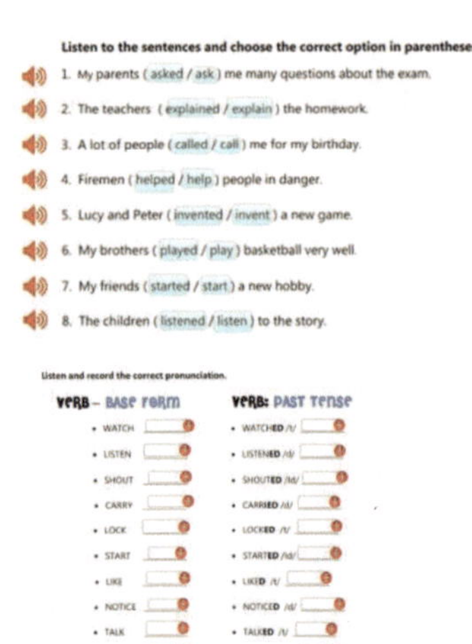

PRONUNCIATION OF S/ES

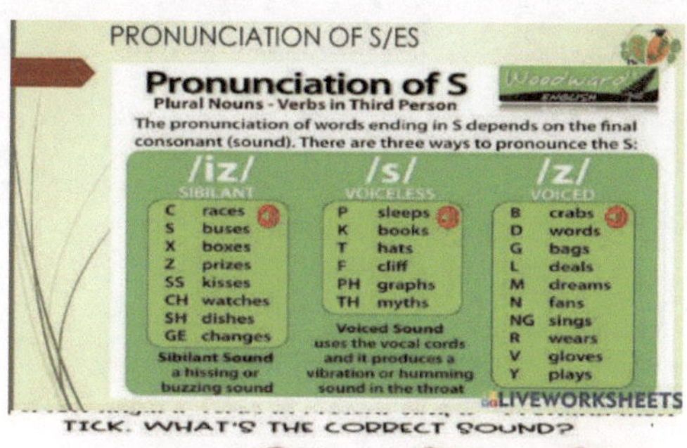

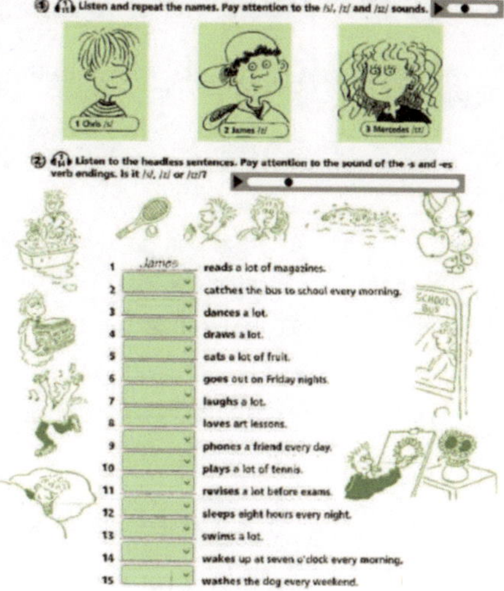

STRESS

WORD STRESS

Choose a word in each question that has different stress pattern.

	A	B	C	D
1	A active	B creative	C friendly	D funny
2	A helpful	B lazy	C quiet	D polite
3	A popular	B parrot	C giraffe	D forest
4	A desert	B mountain	C elephant	D volcano
5	A address	B penguin	C tiger	D picture
6	A helicopter	B motorbike	C underground	D receptionist
7	A tourist	B attractive	C unusual	D biology
8	A chemistry	B comfortable	C geography	D language
9	A history	B design	C physics	D science
10	A technology	B drama	C peaceful	D sofa
11	A valley	B suitcase	C visitor	D invite
12	A volunteer	B different	C difficult	D countryside
13	A complete	B award	C finish	D prepare
14	A happy	B decide	C happen	D practise
15	A piano	B violin	C guitar	D keyboard
16	A basketball	B football	C tennis	D discuss
17	A information	B education	C television	D receptionist
18	A weather	B believe	C because	D prefer
19	A scientist	B favourite	C belong	D holiday
20	A summer	B arrive	C fantastic	D surprise

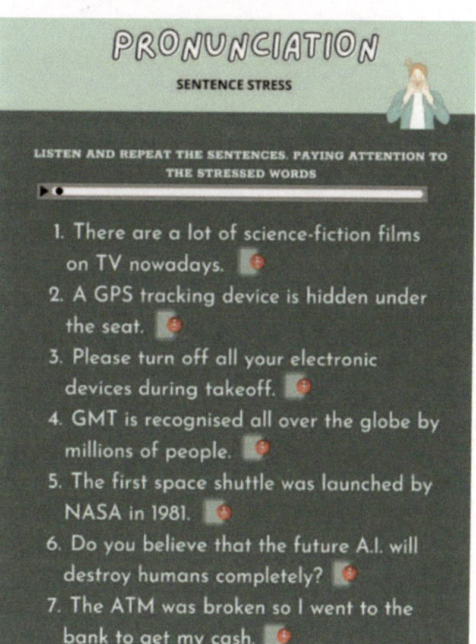

CONNECTED SPEECH: WEAK FORMS

❖ Choose the correct form of the words in **bold**.

1) Which **has** been the best singer on the stage? - I think she **has**.
/hæz/ - /həz/   /hæz/ - /həz/

2) **Does** Sally go to bed early? - Yes, she **does**.
/dəz/ - /dʌz/   /dəz/ - /dʌz/

3) Where **does** Jane buy her clothes?
/dʌz/ - /dəz/

4) **That** is the place I would love to go someday.
/ðæt/ - /ðət/

5) It **is** my dog.
/ɪz/ - /ɪs/

6) 'I **haven't** been to Paris' **that   is** what I told you yesterday.
/hævnt/ - /(h)əvnt/   /ðæt/ - /ðət/   /ɪz/ - /ɪs/

7) **Are** they here?
/ɑː/ - /ə/

❖ Listen and choose the correct form/transcription of the words in **bold**.

▶ **1) Those** animals over there **are** elephants.
/ðəʊz/ - /ðəʊs/   /ɑː/ - /ə/

▶ 2) She **doesn't** know yet, but we **have** prepared a birthday party for her.
/dʌznt/ - /dəznt/   /həv/ - /hæv/

▶ 3) There **are** animals which are incredibly dangerous for human beings.
/ɑː/ - /ə/

▶ 4) I **have** a very beautiful teddy bear in my bedroom.
/həv/ - /hæv/

▶ 5) What is **that**?
/ðæt/ - /ðət/

▶ 6) What, **this** or **these**?
/ðɪs/ - /ðɪz/ /ðɪːz/ - /ðɪs/

▶ 7) I am not sure **that** quarantine is gonna be over anytime soon.
/ðæt/ - /ðət/

▶ 8) **Do** you really think so?
/dʊ-ə/ - /duː/

Annex 8: Pre-test

**This test is not meant to give you a mark. It may help you to find out which sounds and other aspects of English pronunciation could be the most difficult for you.*

QUESTIONS:

[Morpheme "-ed"] Which ending?

1. *Dropped:*   a) /t/   b) /d/   c) /ɪd/   d) /ed/

2. *Called:*   a) /t/   b) /d/   c) /ɪd/   d) /ed/

3. *Visited:*   a) /t/   b) /d/   c) /ɪd/   d) /ed/

[Morpheme "-s"] Which ending?

4. *Horses:*   a) /s/   b) /z/   c) /ɪz/   d) /es/

5. *Cats:*   a) /s/   b) /z/   c) /ɪz/   d) /es/

6. *Dogs:*   a) /s/   b) /z/   c) /ɪz/   d) /es/

[Word stress] Choose the word that is different from the others

7.   a) *items*   b) *column*   c) *number*   d) *alone*

8.   a) *nowhere*   b) *birthday*   c) *mistake*   d) *toilet*

9.   a) *guitar*   b) *eighteen*   c) *English*   d) *today*

[Syllables] Which word has a different number of syllables from the others?

10.   a) *snakes*   b) *sheep*   c) *foxes*   d) *cats*

11.   a) *likes*   b) *wants*   c) *talks*   d) *washes*

12.   a) *wanted*   b) *walked*   c) *saved*   d) *brushed*

13.	a) *hand*	b) *cat*	c) *car*	d) *cap*
14.	a) *calm*	b) *car*	c) *cap*	d) *dance*
15.	a) *come*	b) *son*	c) *sun*	d) *move*
16.	a) *come*	b) *gone*	c) *long*	d) *want*
17.	a) *what*	b) *hot*	c) *most*	d) *salt*
18.	a) *docker*	b) *love*	c) *lock*	d) *strong*
19.	a) *post*	b) *lost*	c) *most*	d) *rose*
20.	a) *hot*	b) *hold*	c) *gone*	d) *swan*

21. /tʃ/	a) *church*	b) *such*	c) *child*	d) *ridge*
22. /ʃ/	a) *sugar*	b) *kiss*	c) *push*	d) *shape*
23. /dʒ/	a) *German*	b) *justice*	c) *chicken*	d) *postage*
24. /j/	a) *yatch*	b) *you*	c) *university*	d) *major*
25. /g/	a) *great*	b) *germs*	c) *pig*	d) *gate*
26. /s/	a) *suit*	b) *nice*	c) *short*	d) *sit*
27. /z/	a) *zoo*	b) *zip*	c) *kiss*	d) *rose*
28. /θ/	a) *think*	b) *mother*	c) *thanks*	d) *thin*
29. /w/	a) *winter*	b) *language*	c) *whole*	d) *wink*
30. /ʒ/	a) *division*	b) *measure*	c) *casual*	d) *brush*

ANSWERS:

[Morpheme "-ed"] **Which ending?**

1. *Dropped:*   a) /t/   b) /d/   c) /ɪd/   d) /ed/

2. *Called:*   a) /t/   b) /d/   c) /ɪd/   d) /ed/

3. *Visited:*   a) /t/   b) /d/   c) /ɪd/   d) /ed/

[Morpheme "-s"] **Which ending?**

4. *Horses:*   a) /s/   b) /z/   c) /ɪz/   d) /es/

5. *Cats:*   a) /s/   b) /z/   c) /ɪz/   d) /es/

6. *Dogs:*   a) /s/   b) /z/   c) /ɪz/   d) /es/

[Word stress] **Choose the word that is different from the others**

7.   a) *items*   b) *column*   c) *number*   d) *alone*

8.   a) *nowhere*   b) *birthday*   c) *mistake*   d) *toilet*

9.   a) *guitar*   b) *eighteen*   c) *English*   d) *today*

[Syllables] **Which word has a different number of syllables from the others?**

10.   a) *snakes*   b) *sheep*   c) *foxes*   d) *cats*

11.   a) *likes*   b) *wants*   c) *talks*   d) *washes*

12.   a) *wanted*   b) *walked*   c) *saved*   d) *brushed*

 Which word doesn't belong? Find the word whose vowel sounds differently

13.   a) *hand*   b) *cat*   c) *car*   d) *cap*

14.   a) *calm*   b) *car*   c) *cap*   d) *dance*

15.   a) *come*   b) *son*   c) *sun*   d) *move*

16.   a) *come*   b) *gone*   c) *long*   d) *want*

17.   a) *what*   b) *hot*   c) *most*   d) *salt*

18.   a) *docker*   b) *love*   c) *lock*   d) *strong*

19.   a) *post*   b) *lost*   c) *most*   d) *rose*

20.   a) *hot*   b) *hold*   c) *gone*   d) *swan*

 Which word doesn't belong? Three of the four words includes the given consonant; find the word whose consonant sounds differently

21. /ʧ/   a) *church*   b) *such*   c) *child*   d) *ridge*

22. /ʃ/   a) *sugar*   b) *kiss*   c) *push*   d) *shape*

23. /dʒ/   a) *German*   b) *justice*   c) *chicken*   d) *postage*

24. /j/   a) *yatch*   b) *you*   c) *university*   d) *major*

25. /g/   a) *great*   b) *germs*   c) *pig*   d) *gate*

26. /s/   a) *suit*   b) *nice*   c) *short*   d) *sit*

27. /z/   a) *zoo*   b) *zip*   c) *kiss*   d) *rose*

28. /θ/   a) *think*   b) *mother*   c) *thanks*   d) *thin*

29. /w/   a) *winter*   b) *language*   c) *whole*   d) *wink*

30. /ʒ/   a) *division*   b) *measure*   c) *casual*   d) *brush*

Diciembre, 2023